Harvard
Business
Review

on

FINDING &
KEEPING THE
BEST PEOPLE

The Harvard Business Review
paperback series

If you need the best practices and ideas for the business challenges you face—but don't have time to find them—*Harvard Business Review* **paperbacks** are for you. Each book is a collection of HBR's inspiring and useful perspectives on a given management topic, all in one place.

The titles include:

Harvard Business Review on Advancing Your Career
Harvard Business Review on Aligning Technology with
    Strategy
Harvard Business Review on Building Better Teams
Harvard Business Review on Collaborating Effectively
Harvard Business Review on Communicating Effectively
Harvard Business Review on Finding & Keeping the Best
    People
Harvard Business Review on Fixing Health Care from
    Inside & Out
Harvard Business Review on Greening Your Business
    Profitably
Harvard Business Review on Increasing Customer Loyalty
Harvard Business Review on Inspiring & Executing
    Innovation
Harvard Business Review on Making Smart Decisions
Harvard Business Review on Managing Supply Chains
Harvard Business Review on Rebuilding Your Business Model
Harvard Business Review on Reinventing Your Marketing
Harvard Business Review on Succeeding As an Entrepreneur
Harvard Business Review on Thriving in Emerging Markets
Harvard Business Review on Winning Negotiations

Harvard Business Review

on

FINDING & KEEPING THE BEST PEOPLE

Harvard Business Review Press

Boston, Massachusetts

Library of Congress Cataloging-in-Publication Data
Harvard business review on finding & keeping the best people.
    p. cm.—(Harvard business review paperback)
    ISBN 978-1-4221-6254-5 (alk. paper) 1. Employees—Recruiting.
2. Employee retention. 3. Personnel management. I. Harvard
business review. II. Title: Harvard business review on finding and
keeping the best people.
    HF5549.5.R44H2873 2011
    658.3'11—dc22
                                                        2010054385

Contents

**Harvard
Business
Review**

on

FINDING &
KEEPING THE
BEST PEOPLE

The Definitive Guide to Recruiting in Good Times and Bad

by Claudio Fernández-Aráoz,
Boris Groysberg, and Nitin Nohria

WHEN ECONOMIC CRISIS HITS AND companies focus on cutting costs—or on their very survival—they slash hiring. But if history is any guide, in the first few months after the upheaval subsides, hiring quickly becomes a front-burner issue.

Consider the period following the terrorist attacks of September 11, 2001, when the economic outlook appeared dire. In rapid succession, the U.S. initiated the war in Afghanistan, Enron's house of cards fell, other corporate scandals ensued, the SARS scare struck Asia, and the Iraq War began. The economy was in recession, and struggling firms retained only their strongest people. But even before things turned a corner in 2003, the smarter and abler companies—having cleaned house and discovered what was missing from their talent pools—took advantage of the buyer's market and began staffing for the future. By June 2003, the war for talent was on again in full force, and companies hired aggressively until the economy went into a tailspin in 2008.

History will again repeat itself. Even now, before the recession lifts, our research suggests that most global companies are running into staffing problems in emerging markets, and they are also having a difficult time finding talented younger managers to replace baby boom retirees. These problems will be made all the worse because, we've found, current hiring practices are haphazard at best and ineffective at worst. And even when companies find the right people, they have difficulty retaining them.

This article offers our best thinking about the most effective way to hire top-level managers, based on a combination of our own and established research about the relationship between recruiting and long-term corporate performance (see the research sidebar). The following is, to our knowledge, the first time that an end-to-end set of best practices has been put forward in one place. Our compendium comprises seven steps, which cover the full recruitment spectrum: anticipating the need for new hires, specifying the job, developing a pool of candidates, assessing the candidates, closing the deal, integrating the newcomer, and reviewing the effectiveness of the hiring process.

The focus of our research was on recruiting at the top three levels of organizations—C-level executives, their

Idea in Brief

Recessions present an unexpected opportunity for companies to snap up the top-level talent needed to drive growth in better times. But most firms squander this opportunity because their recruitment practices are scattershot.

To capture the best talent now *and* retain your stars once the recession eases, you'll need a rigorous recruitment process that includes these steps:

- Anticipate your future leadership needs, based on your strategic business plan. Intuit's deep analysis of long-term staffing needs has contributed to famously smooth management transitions.

- Identify the specific competencies required in each position you need to fill. For example, ask, "Does this job require an entrepreneur, manager, or leader?"

- Develop a sufficiently large candidate pool. Considering both inside and outside candidates increases the likelihood you'll find the right person for each job.

direct reports, and the layer below that. We call this the "top-*x* group," where *x* is the number of senior executives constituting the critical leadership pool in the company. The size of this pool can vary from 20 to 50 people in a midsized organization to as many as 1,000 in a large multinational. We are primarily concerned with external recruiting, although our findings can be applied to internal hiring efforts as well.

Of course, any leader currently faced with the unhappy prospect of downsizing may find it difficult to think about staffing right now. But whatever the future brings, firms that learn to hire talent and retain it successfully will have a distinct advantage in the years ahead.

Idea in Practice

Steps to effective recruiting:

Anticipate Your Needs

Every two to three years review your high-level leadership requirements in light of your strategic business plan. Answer these questions:

- How many people will we need, in what positions, in the next few years?
- What will the organizational structure look like?
- What must our leadership pipeline contain today to ensure that we find and develop tomorrow's leaders?

Specify the Job

For each leadership position you've identified, specify competencies needed in that role. For example:

- Job-based: What capabilities will the job require?
- Team-based: Will the applicant need to manage political dynamics?

- Firm-based: What resources (supporting talent, technology) will the organization need to provide the person who fills this role?

Develop the Pool

Cast your net widely for candidates by asking suppliers, customers, board members, professional service providers, and trusted insiders for suggestions. Consider "inside-outsiders" (internal candidates not bound by corporate tradition and ideology) and "outside-insiders" (former employees, customers, suppliers, advisers, or anyone who's worked closely with a trusted insider).

Assess the Candidates

Have each candidate's prospective boss, boss's supervisor, and the top HR manager conduct "behavioral event interviews": Ask candidates to describe experiences they've had that resemble situations

Hiring Gets a Failing Grade

Most companies react to hiring situations as emergencies; that might explain why so many do it so poorly. When we surveyed 50 CEOs of global companies, along with a pool of executive search consultants who rated about they'll face in your organization. Probe for exact actions candidates took and the reasoning they followed.

Evaluate a broad spectrum of references—former bosses, peers, and direct reports—asking about specific things candidates did and actual results achieved.

Close the Deal

Once you've settled on your final choice of candidate, boost the chances your job offer will be accepted:

- Share your passion about the company and the position, showing genuine interest in the candidate.

- Acknowledge the role's opportunities *and* challenges, differentiating the opportunities at your firm from those of competitors.

- Strike a creative balance between salary, bonus, and other long-term incentives.

Integrate the Newcomer

Integrate new hires into your company's culture:

- During their first few months, have bosses and the HR manager check in regularly with each new recruit.

- Assign each newcomer a mentor—an established star in your organization. Mentors should provide ongoing support, not just an initial "buddy" fix to help newcomers feel at home.

- During newcomers' meetings with mentors, bosses, and HR, explore questions such as: Are we providing you with enough support? What other types of support would be useful? Can you describe the relationships you've developed throughout the organization? What other types of relationships would you find useful?

500 firms, we found hiring practices to be disturbingly vague: Respondents relied heavily on subjective personal preferences or on largely unquestioned organizational traditions, often based on false assumptions.

The executives we surveyed held widely differing views regarding the desirable attributes of new hires.

Our Research

OUR RESEARCH IS BASED ON two major studies. The first, conducted throughout 2007, included interviews with 50 CEOs of major global companies, followed by interviews with their HR managers and a quantitative survey of their current HR practices. Participating companies collectively employed about 3 million people, earned more than $1 trillion in yearly revenues, and had a market cap of about $2 trillion. All major sectors were represented, including industrial, high-technology, life sciences, financial services, consumer products, and service businesses. Likewise, all relevant geographic regions were covered, including North America; Latin America; the UK, Germany, and France; the Middle East; India and China; and Australia.

The second study was a survey of executive-search consultants, conducted in the summer and fall of 2008. Respondents rated the talent-management practices of about 500 companies. Sixty-seven percent of those who responded had over 10 years of experience in recruitment, and 59% had specialized in a given industry for 10 years or more. The survey was designed to create a broad-based view of the state of the art in selection, hiring, integration, and talent management practices.

The article is also built on the research conducted by Claudio Fernández-Aráoz for the book, *Great People Decisions* (Wiley 2007) and by Boris Groysberg, Andrew N. McLean, and Nitin Nohria for the May 2006 HBR article "Are Leaders Portable?" Finally, we conducted a major review of academic articles about selection and hiring.

They emphatically disagreed on whether it was best to hire insiders or outsiders, on who should be involved in the recruiting process, on what assessment tools were most suitable, and on what the keys were to successful hiring and retention.

Furthermore, 43% of the executive search consultants reported that their client companies considered the number of years of relevant work experience to be one of the top reasons for hiring a particular candidate, whereas only 24% gave similar weight to the ability to collaborate in teams—and an alarmingly small 11% factored in a candidate's readiness to learn new things. In today's increasingly turbulent business and economic landscape, in which, as one of us likes to put it, "even the past has become unpredictable," we find this neglect of a potential candidate's adaptability mystifying.

Assessment practices were equally variable (even within the same company). On one end of the scale, in 32% of companies, candidates for senior positions went through only one to five interviews; at the other end, 12% of firms subjected candidates to 21 or more. Shockingly, only half of the top-x managers recruited were interviewed by anyone in the C-suite. Fully half the companies relied primarily on the hiring manager's gut feel, selecting a candidate believed to have "what it took" to be successful in any job. What's more, we found that companies based their hiring decisions mainly on interview performance, paying relatively little attention to careful reference checks.

Given the ad hoc quality, lack of specified criteria, and inconsistency of practices among the companies we studied, it's no wonder that usually about a third of promising new hires depart within three years of being recruited.

It's one thing to take a poor approach to hiring. But what really stuns us is that many CEOs do not recognize their recruiting situation for what it is; some are even ignorant of their company's own demographic projections mandating aggressive hiring to replace soon-to-be-retiring managers. Even those who recognize the looming shortage of talent are ill-prepared to fill it.

So what it comes down to is this: Despite a universal acknowledgment that hiring good people is a key source of competitive advantage, we could find only a few companies that excel at one or more aspects of the hiring process and just a handful—most notably Southwest Airlines, McKinsey, Intuit, TCS, and ServiceMaster—that come anywhere close to a hiring "gold standard." On the whole, there is neither a generally accepted code of best practices for hiring for senior-level positions nor a single company that demonstrates true best practices along each step of the process.

Clearly, organizations need to take a serious look at the challenges facing them. They need to stop treating recruitment as a big surprise. They have to approach hiring from a rigorous, strategic, and objective point of view. They must develop best practices, which in many cases will mean drastically revamping their hiring processes. They need to educate their line managers so they can hire effectively. And they have to ensure that their HR managers provide the right support. Let's walk through each step of the process, with challenges and best practices in mind.

Step 1: Anticipate the Need

When we asked the CEOs in the 50 major global companies to forecast their revenues for the next three years, most had little trouble. Some even broke down projected revenues from as-yet-undeveloped products and services by geographic region. But these same executives had difficulty making similar predictions for the size and composition of their top-x groups, even with the help of their HR heads. Although most reported that they'd like to see a broader diversity of nationality, gender, and entrepreneurial experience in their senior managers, few had translated these aspirations into a concrete and proactive hiring plan. In fact, few had any strategic talent plan to complement their admirably detailed business plan.

The first step in establishing a sound recruitment process is to recognize that your firm's existing top-x pool is probably inadequate. Despite your best efforts, some top talent will leave to pursue other opportunities. And certain kinds of talent—like experienced executives in emerging markets—may not be available, so you may need to hire and then develop promising people.

Organizations should, at the very least, review their high-level leadership requirements every two to three years and develop a plan that can answer the following questions: How many people will we need, in what positions, in the next few years? What qualities are we looking for in those people, and how will we know when we find them? What will the organizational structure look like? What does our pipeline need to contain today to ensure that we can find, develop, and support the leaders of tomorrow?

One firm that excels in this area is Intuit—the software company best known for products like QuickBooks and TurboTax. Taking a page from the best analytics

Hiring top executives: a comprehensive end-to-end process

	Poor practices	Best practices	Implementation challenges
1. Anticipate the need	• Hiring only when you have an opening • Having an ad hoc succession plan • Overlooking the skills your organization will need in the future • Indulging in irrational optimism about attrition, succession depth, and recruiting yields	• Conducting ongoing, proactive analysis of future needs • Continually evaluating the pool of potential talent • Developing rigorous periodic forecasts of the company's talent needs	• Linking your talent plan to your strategic plan • Incorporating input from HR professionals into the strategic-planning process
2. Specify the job	• Relying on generic competency models • Looking primarily for charisma, general ability, and track record	• Defining the specific demands of the job • Specifying which skills and experience are relevant • Identifying the team the candidate will need to work with or recruit • Considering how company culture and context affect the role	• Ensuring a close dialogue between HR and top management • Building up-front consensus among key decision makers about job requirements
3. Develop the pool	• Taking a scatter-shot, ad hoc approach to finding candidates • Limiting the pool	• Developing a large pool • Including insiders, outsiders, inside-outsiders, and outside-insiders	• Transcending organizational silos

	Poor practices	Best practices	Implementation challenges
	• Looking for only external candidates or only internal candidates	• Considering people on the periphery of the organization (employees in remote offices, consultants, suppliers, customers)	• Encouraging open discussion at the top about when and how to conduct external talent searches
		• Tapping your networks and involving the right external partners	
		• Asking candidates' peers for nominations	
4. Assess the candidates	• Settling on the first adequate choice • Looking endlessly for the perfect choice • Going with your gut only • Using the wrong interviewers • Including too many unreliable filters and bureaucratic steps • Employing unstructured or generic interviews • Conducting inadequate (or no) reference checks	• Using a small number of high-caliber, well-trained, properly motivated interviewers • Employing rigorous behavioral event interviews • Conducting detailed reference checks • Including top stakeholders in candidate assessment	• Educating and training senior line managers in interview techniques • Ensuring the right level of involvement of both HR and the relevant line managers
5. Close the deal	• Assuming money is everything	• Demonstrating active support for the candidate's interests	• Ensuring commitment of top managers to closing the deal

(continued)

Hiring top executives: a comprehensive end-to-end process (continued)

	Poor practices	Best practices	Implementation challenges
	• Showing too little commitment to the candidate's success • Discussing only the positives of the job • Failing to involve C-level in discussions	• Describing the job realistically • Involving the hiring manager personally, not just HR, in closing the deal • Ensuring that compensation is fair to other employees • Involving C-level for top positions	• Ensuring compensation equity
6. Integrate the newcomer	• Assuming the new hire is "plug and play" • Providing inadequate support and mentoring	• Using veteran top performers as mentors • Making sure the newcomer checks in regularly with boss, mentor, and HR, even when no problems have arisen	• Providing adequate ramp-up time • Rewarding mentors
7. Audit and review	• Hanging on to bad hires • Failing to review hiring practices and institutionalize the best ones	• Removing bad hires within the first year • Regularly reviewing recruiting practices • Identifying and rewarding excellent interviewers • Holding all assessors accountable for the quality of their evaluations	• Institutionalizing audit and review • Being willing to admit mistakes, learn, and move on

practices of Harrah's (see "Diamonds in the Data Mine," HBR May 2003), Intuit has built a proprietary database that combines information from various hiring pipelines (such as internal-mobility figures, employee-referral programs, and external-recruiting yields) with additional data on anticipated attrition and business unit budgets to predict how many people, including top executives, will be needed annually throughout the organization. In this way, Intuit has been able to correctly predict more than 90% of its talent needs, which has greatly reduced its recruiting costs and smoothed its employee transitions.

Step 2: Specify the Job

Most companies rely on a leadership competency model to help define the attributes they want in their managers. These models typically emphasize generic leadership skills, such as strategic thinking and articulating a vision, as well as abstract character traits like courage, humility, and drive. Combine these ideals with industry experience and a proven track record, so the thinking goes, and you have a perfect leader.

The problem, of course, is that there's no such thing. If a new high-level executive is to be more than a flash in the pan, a company must define the particular job skills it needs, and recruit and judge candidates accordingly. The May 2006 HBR article "Are Leaders Portable?" laid out a systematic way to consider the full range of skills that a high-level job would require, called the "portfolio model of human capital." Our research suggests that hiring is greatly improved if companies employ the model's basic tenets as a template:

Job-Based Competencies

What specific capabilities will this job require over the next few years? Will the focus be on growth or on engineering a turnaround? Does it require someone who is fundamentally an entrepreneur, a manager, or a leader? If this is a stretch opportunity, can the candidate grow into the job? What are the next jobs he or she is likely to move into, and what capabilities may be required for those positions?

Team-Based Competencies

Does the candidate have the skills to lead his or her prospective team, and how do they overlap with other members' skills? How will the applicant manage resistance or political dynamics? Will the individual need to hire additional people to build out the team? If so, can he or she bring in other talented executives?

Firm-Based Competencies

How well will the candidate fit into the organizational culture? Will this person flourish with the resources (supporting talent, technology, organizational reputation, and so on) the organization can provide? If the person comes from a more resource-rich environment, can equivalent support be provided, or at least can the candidate be helped to adapt to less?

Step 3: Develop the Pool

You'd think it would be obvious that the wider you cast your net, the greater the likelihood of finding the right person for the job. But in fact, research from the Center for Creative Leadership has shown, nearly a quarter of the time (one in four cases!) the executive selected was the only candidate considered. That's a pity, for in talking to many prospects companies gain valuable information about ways different people would tackle the job, and they benefit from thinking afresh in each case about which skills the job truly calls for.

In casting that net, it's important to include a group that Joseph Bower in a November 2007 HBR article called "inside-outsiders." These are internal candidates who are nevertheless not bound by corporate tradition and ideology and so may have a more objective view of the organization. A likely prospect might come from an international branch or may manage a line outside the company's main field. The CEO of a multinational bank told us that he was particularly proud of having promoted some expatriates who had been "forgotten" by the organization.

By extension, another category of candidate to include is the "outside-insider"—that is, a former employee; a customer, supplier, or adviser to the firm; or someone who has worked closely with a trusted insider. Any top-x search, then, needs to contain a mix of insiders, inside-outsiders, outside-insiders, and true outsiders.

The most effective strategy for sourcing is to think not only about candidates themselves but also about people who may know the best ones. Rather than waste your time calling too many irrelevant prospects, talk to individuals who are likely to suggest several high-quality candidates right off the bat. The best leads will come from suppliers, customers, board members, professional service providers, and the like. Amgen CEO Kevin Sharer puts out an "all points bulletin" whenever he's looking for senior talent—reaching out to recruiting firms, consultants he has used, industry associates, and board members. This strategy helps him identify great candidates and also find further contacts who can connect him with new prospects. As effective as this approach is, we've found few CEOs and senior executives who get as systematically and personally involved as Sharer does in the generation of candidates.

This network-sourcing strategy is equally powerful for internal candidates. Research studying the career paths of middle-management executives at one *Fortune* 100 firm, for instance, found that 14% of the people ranked by their peers as being in the top 30% (in terms of potential) rose to become corporate officers. Conversely, only 2% of those ranked in the bottom 70% did so. In other words, those ranked as high potentials by their peers were seven times more likely to make it to the top.

Additionally, we have observed that organizations are often extremely poor at promoting high-potential candidates across divisions, so it's important to make a special effort to break through silos to identify promising inside-outsiders working in other units.

How do you know when to stop looking for candidates? Surprising as this may sound, it has been demonstrated both empirically and theoretically—whether one is searching for CFO or a mate—that the simple decision rule of "meeting a dozen" will work well, even when you are sampling candidates from a very large population. Once you have 10 to 12 carefully generated, high-quality candidates, you should move to the next step.

Step 4: Assess the Candidates

A few decades ago, a number of consumer goods companies applied mathematical models to quantify the expected value of their advertising investments. These same models can be applied to assess the effectiveness of the recruiting process. They allow you to quantify the expected profitability of investing in generating more candidates, improving your assessments, reducing the compensation of hired candidates, and reducing the operating costs of your recruiting practices.

The most important finding from the application of these models is that improving the quality of assessments is three times more profitable than increasing the size of the candidate pool—and six times more profitable than getting the chosen candidate to accept a lower compensation package. A good assessment yields more than a good candidate—it can actually improve the company's bottom line and market value in a very significant way. Specifically, a company can increase its yearly profits and market value by about a third through the disciplined generation and assessment of candidates for a CEO position. The typical cost of a search (with or without professional external recruiters) is negligible when compared with the expected return on investment in candidate assessment. Even for a small company—say, one with a market value of $100 million—a 10% improvement in the quality of candidate assessments would have an expected return of almost $2 million in additional profits per year and mean an increase in market value of $30 million to $40 million.

Of course, if judging people accurately were an easy task, there would be no need for executive search consultants (or, perhaps, divorce lawyers). Assessing people for complex positions is inherently difficult for several reasons, including the unique and changing characteristics of many jobs, the challenge of assessing intangible traits, and the time constraints of many candidates.

To complicate things even further, what is usually called the "assessment process" is in reality three separate practices, with three different objectives. One goal is to evaluate the candidates. A second is to sell the position and the organization to highly attractive candidates, especially those who may be wary. A third is to build organizational consensus on the suitability of the new candidate, particularly if he or she is external.

Each of these objectives can conflict with the other two. Too stringent a focus on assessment can leave a candidate feeling judged and unenthusiastic about the firm. Too great an emphasis on selling may make candidates feel that you are desperate and that they are in a position to drive a tough bargain. Too hard a push toward consensus by involving layers and layers of people and many interview stages invites internal politicking—and may also drive away attractive candidates whose schedules, or need for confidentiality, won't allow for a lengthy decision process. Avoiding these pitfalls requires the following four elements.

The Right Interviewers

A robust assessment process follows a sequence of steps. We believe that the first is to select a small number of individuals—typically the hire's prospective boss, the boss's boss, and the top HR manager—to conduct the interviews and check references. It's critical to note that *it's more important to choose the right assessors than to focus on the assessment technique.* Getting the wrong people involved in your hiring process increases the risk not only of hiring an unsuitable candidate but also of rejecting a good candidate. The worst interviewers actually have a slightly *negative* effect—that is, following their recommendations will lead to a worse decision than simply hiring a candidate from the pool at random.

There are a host of reasons why this might be so. Interviewers may enter into the process with the wrong motives: Some people, for example, don't like to surround themselves with strong, high-potential colleagues. Interviewers may also be subject to a whole series of unconscious psychological biases, including a bias toward people like themselves. Interviewers who are themselves weak managers, for instance, may rate highly candidates who are weak in the same way they are and, worse, rate strong managers as poor simply because they are different.

The best interviewers are deeply familiar with the range of experience and skills the position requires and are sufficiently self-confident to look for the best possible candidates, even those they may deem more talented than themselves. They possess a high level of emotional intelligence and the ability to decode nonverbal behavior. They are masters of self-control—and great listeners. Of course, it's difficult to find individuals who can fit this bill, so companies have a choice. They can "empower the knowledgeable"—those who already demonstrate some of these skills and have been educated and trained in assessment (possibly because they work in HR). Or they can follow an even more promising strategy, which is to "educate the powerful"—that is, make sure senior managers and executives are properly educated in making great people decisions.

The Right Number of Interviewers

Given the importance and difficulty of assessments, you may naturally be tempted to involve a large number of interviewers. That, however, would be the wrong strategy in today's world, where exceptional talent has become scarce. The greater the number of filters you include in an interview process (in which, for example, each successive interviewer can eliminate a candidate), the more you reduce your risk of hiring the wrong person—but also the more you increase your risk of rejecting the right one. Probabilistic analysis shows that three independent top-caliber interviewers are enough. With the right skills and motivation, they will help you reach a high level of accuracy in your assessments while still maintaining a low probability of losing exceptional talents.

The Right Techniques

Properly structured interviews and reference checks will help you achieve reliable assessments. We recommend a particular type of structured interview, called a "behavioral event interview," followed by thorough reference checks that fill out the picture.

Behavioral event interviews are far more effective than unstructured interviews or those in which standard and general questions are asked about a candidate's strengths or weaknesses. With some training and practice, even an intelligent novice can master the basics. The interviewer should ask candidates to describe specific experiences they've had that are similar to situations they'll be facing in your organization. For example, you might say, "Describe a time when you needed to work under an intense deadline," or "Tell me about a situation in which you managed conflicting interests among your colleagues," or "Explain how you saw a new product through to completion." The assessor should probe for details of the candidate's exact actions and reasoning at the time. The candidate should not be allowed to discuss hypothetical scenarios or make vague statements about what "we" did. The objective is to find out whether the individual's past reveals the specific competencies you're looking for.

After the assessments have been completed, it's important for the interviewers to come together and have a rigorous, disciplined conversation about the evidence. This conversation should not be allowed to veer off into vague discussions of overall impressions or of how well everyone hit it off with the candidate. Some companies that excel at recruiting require all interviewers to score candidates on a matrix of specific attributes. They then tabulate the data and gather to review their combined ratings, explore differences in their judgments, and arrive at a consensus on which candidates should be finalists. This process naturally results in a bias against including any candidate about whom a strong consensus cannot be reached.

Given the fallibility of memory and the human tendency to overestimate one's own ability and achievements while being interviewed, it's important to balance interviews with formal reference checks once the initial pool has been reduced to a few strong finalists. In general you will want a broad spectrum of references. A boss in a former job can attest to how well a candidate can think strategically or get results. Former peers can discuss the candidate's ability to influence and collaborate. And former direct reports can reveal leadership traits. Again, ask about specific things the candidate did, particular tactics chosen, and actual results achieved, so you can put his or her attributes and achievements into a day-to-day context. You should go out of your way to get permission from the finalists to speak with truly relevant people, not just their friends.

At this later stage, a candidate risks less and has more to gain in giving permission for such assessments.

There is an art to getting referees—who may be loath to say disparaging things about their colleagues—to speak frankly. Asking specific questions is one safeguard. In addition, you should point out that it does no one any good if the candidate gets hired but then fails. You could also add that of course no one is perfect, and honest replies will help in integrating the successful candidate into the job. Finally, if the position is senior and the reference is critical, a top executive should meet in person with the referee.

The Right Organizational Support

Once you are convinced that you have one to three highly qualified candidates, it's time to start exposing the finalists to a few key stakeholders who have been properly briefed about the position's requirements. It's important here to ensure that these people hold no conflicts of interest and can evaluate the candidates objectively. They should review each prospect's relevant skills, as well as the detailed assessments, to avoid rejecting the right candidates for the wrong reasons.

How does that happen? First of all, people commonly assume that an impressive educational background or years of experience in senior positions at a great company are almost a guarantee for success on the job. GE alumni, for instance, are usually thought to do very well as CEOs elsewhere. They all have great academic credentials, and of course GE is a factory of senior talent.

But when they didn't have the right mix of competencies needed for the specific jobs they were hired to do, a number have actually destroyed significant value when becoming CEOs of other companies.

Second, many people fall into the first-impression bias and very rapidly (in a matter of minutes, or even seconds) reach a conclusion, pro or con, about the candidate, based on snap judgments. As a result, during most of the interview they just seek selective confirmatory information from the candidate's background rather than keeping an open mind. And, third, it's possible that an interviewer does not conduct the search in good faith for political reasons.

Ideally, once they're satisfied that the finalists have been selected for the right reasons, the three principals (the boss, the boss's boss, and the HR executive) should reach a consensus on who is the best of the finalists. Ultimately though, the direct boss is the one who should make the final decision. Every manager should have the right to hire and fire—and of course be accountable for his or her decisions.

Step 5: Close the Deal

Having found the candidate of their dreams, too many companies fail to close the deal. If you are ambitious enough to try to attract the best candidates, at least one out of five will be likely to turn down your offer. And the situation is even more intense in the most attractive growth markets, such as China and India, where the talent pools are extremely limited for their size and growth rates. There, candidates are blessed with options; we frequently hear of individuals receiving three, and even four, job offers.

What factors determine whether or not the top candidate will accept your offer?

The Organization's Commitment

Many executives in our survey think financial compensation is the linchpin in recruiting. But closing the deal is not just about money; it's also about demonstrating to candidates that the organization is committed to their success. No high performer wants to take a new job only to be demoted, downsized, or left to flounder in organizational quagmires. A personal show of commitment by the CEO is essential: By taking the time to share his or her passion about the company and the position with the candidate, by expressing a sincere interest in the project and the person, and by genuinely understanding the candidate's motivation, concerns, and long-term fit with the organization, the CEO can send a powerful message that the company cares.

The Job

In their desire to close the deal, many managers present only the positive aspects of the job. This is a mistake, for research shows that a realistic presentation of both the opportunities and the challenges of a prospective position results in higher offer-acceptance rates, better post-employment job satisfaction, and lower turnover. Candidates want to decide for themselves whether they will be able to cope with the challenges they may face.

This doesn't mean dwelling on the downside. To communicate the positives, a successful hiring manager could borrow a page from John F. Kennedy's playbook and ask not only what the candidate can do for the job but what the job can do for the candidate—and then take whatever steps are necessary to make sure the job holds that potential. Managers should also clearly differentiate the opportunities at their firm from those of competitors. The value proposition might range from flexible job design and job rotation to nonfinancial benefits, advantages in the culture, and growth and development opportunities.

The Boss

It's well known that employees do not leave jobs; they leave their managers. Inept managers not only do their own jobs badly, they also destroy the performance (and potential) of the people around them. In their book *Hard Facts, Dangerous Half-Truths & Total Nonsense,* Jeffrey Pfeffer and Robert Sutton review the research on organizational climate over the past half century. They found that "60% to 75% of the employees in any organization—no matter when or where the survey was completed and no matter what occupational group was involved—report that the worst or most stressful aspect of their job is their immediate supervisor."

"Abusive and incompetent management," Pfeffer and Sutton continue, "create billions of dollars of lost productivity each year." And study after study, they conclude, "demonstrates that bad leaders destroy the health, happiness, loyalty, and productivity of their subordinates." Because of this, the hiring manager must demonstrate commitment by being heavily involved in the closing stage of the hiring process, rather than delegating this last, critical step to HR.

Compensation

How much should you pay to get the best candidate? Aside from considering the comparable market rate for the position and the prospect's past salary, there is another important benchmark—the current state of compensation within the company. If you break the bank on an outside person and the amount is discovered, existing staff can feel devalued and demotivated. It's also important to structure the new employee's compensation with an eye not only to immediate effort but also to sustained performance. This goal usually calls, of course, for striking a creative balance among salary, bonus, and long-term incentives, such as restricted shares.

Step 6: Integrate the Newcomer

The recruitment process doesn't end after the deal has been closed, although most companies think it does. Our research shows that many firms take no steps at all to ensure that new employees are integrated into the company's culture. Many hire experienced professionals, expecting them to be "plug and play." Typically, the entire integration "strategy" consists essentially of signing up the promising candidate, making the necessary introductions, and hoping for the best.

But talented new hires should not be given the freedom to sink or swim; more often than not, they sink. We found that 40% of new C-level hires who departed within two years did so because of integration difficulties. Turnover was highest in positions requiring the greatest level of integration. (The COO, for example, is far more dependent on establishing relationships throughout the company than is either the CTO or the CFO.) Similarly, a fall 2007 survey of 2,000 HR and training executives conducted by Novations Group found that a third of employers lost between 10% and 25% of all new employees within the first year. The main reasons respondents gave for employees' departures were (in order of importance): the company's unrealistic expectations, failure to grasp how things get done around the organization, poor communication with immediate supervisors, failure to develop a sense of belonging and purpose, inadequate technical skills, not understanding the link between their job and the organization, and failure to connect with key employees.

In general, organizations that systematically integrate new employees enjoy lower turnover, and the recruits report greater commitment and job satisfaction. The most successful firms move quickly on several fronts to orient newcomers to their own departments and to other parts of the firm. Such companies begin integrating new hires during the interview stage, before they ever come to work. In the first few months, these organizations make sure the boss and HR manager check in regularly with each new recruit, just to see if everything is going well. In some organizations, detailed integration plans are developed similar to those used for acquisitions, complete with specific milestones and backed up by regular progress reports.

The best firms assign each new top-x a mentor, usually an established star in the organization. A veteran of the company's culture can serve as a valuable reality check until the newcomer becomes fully culturally literate. We recommend that companies identify and secure commitment from strong potential mentors before a new hire is brought on board. The mentor's role should be understood to be ongoing, not just a quick "buddy" fix to make the newcomer feel at home. Organizations should mandate that new leaders formally check in quarterly with their mentors, their bosses, and HR for the first year or so, no matter how well they're performing. They should analyze progress against expectations by asking four basic questions: Is the new hire getting adequate support? Is he or she developing the right relationships within the organization? Does the new manager understand the business model? Is there evidence of progress? In the absence of regularly scheduled check-ins, a new hire might be reluctant to ask for help, for fear of losing face. It's important that mentors be trained to give feedback and handle difficult conversations appropriately—that is, to be coaches rather than cheerleaders.

Step 7: Audit and Review

A great recruiting and integration process will minimize, but can never eliminate, the chances of making a hiring mistake. When that happens, best-practice firms act quickly to remove bad hires—that is, within the first year. One year may not be enough time for a new executive hire to forge any great successes—but it's plenty of time to demonstrate ineptitude.

To improve what might be called your "hiring batting average," it's important to regularly audit and review your recruiting practices. Some of the best IT-software companies—including the Indian firms Infosys, TCS, and Wipro—take auditing and review of all their recruiting practices as seriously as they do oversight of their financial systems.

In addition to evaluating your new hires, try to find out what happened to the other internal and external finalists. Though it's hard to tell how the candidates who were not hired might have fared had they come on board, it's still instructive to see how well they're performing in their current roles relative to the candidate who got the job. Does this comparison give you confidence in your decision—or give you pause?

Periodic reviews can also help identify those in your organization who are particularly adept at assessing talent. In fact, rewarding your assessors (and, conversely, holding them accountable) for the quality of their evaluations will motivate them to improve next time.

Companies can and must do better at filling top executive positions than they have up to now. Our hope is that, by following the recommendations we've laid out in these pages, organizations will be able to set the bar higher, reevaluate their recruiting processes, and make "talent management" a reality rather than an empty phrase.

CLAUDIO FERNÁNDEZ-ARÁOZ is a senior adviser at the global executive search firm Egon Zehnder International. **BORIS GROYSBERG** is an associate professor and **NITIN NOHRIA** is the Richard P. Chapman Professor of Business Administration at Harvard Business School.

Originally published in May 2009. Reprint R0905F

Winning the Race for Talent in Emerging Markets

by Douglas A. Ready, Linda A. Hill, and Jay A. Conger

WITH ECONOMIC ACTIVITY IN EMERGING markets growing at compounded rates of around 40%—as compared with 2% to 5% in the West and Japan—it's little wonder that many companies are pegging their prospects for growth to Brazil, Russia, India, and China (BRIC) and, increasingly, other developing nations. Businesses based all over the globe are feverishly competing for people who, often for the first time in their lives, have numerous options and high expectations. Not even companies with established global experience can coast on past success in meeting their staffing needs.

One might assume, for instance, that Standard Chartered Bank, whose heritage dates back to the 1850s in India, Hong Kong, and Singapore, could easily maintain a lead in the race for Asian talent. But just a couple of years ago SCB's China division was unable to find seasoned managers to lead the bank's retail and commercial banking operations. In the words of Hemant Mishr, the head of corporate global sales, "These people and the generations that preceded them have known nothing but poverty and the lack of opportunity. Yet we expect them to be patient, loyal soldiers, and to advance at an orderly pace. It is time to get real. It is their time now."

All three of us have spent decades studying talent management and leadership development, but this war for talent is like nothing we've ever seen before. We recently completed an eight-month research project that involved interviewing dozens of executives and collecting data from more than 20 global companies. Our goal was to identify the factors that differentiate the successful from the less so in emerging markets, and our first analysis revealed four: brand, opportunity, purpose, and culture. These may sound somewhat generic—and logical in any talent market—but they play out in developing nations in particular ways.

Employees in the developing world aren't used to thinking about the future in expansive terms. Now they can look beyond simply making a living. They are particularly attuned to *brand*, for instance, because a desirable affiliation may lead to personal advancement—especially when the brand is associated with inspirational leadership, the kind that challenges employees to develop themselves as leaders and to help build a great company that plays on a global stage.

Not surprisingly, *opportunity* means much the same in the developed and developing worlds: challenging

Idea in Brief

What motivates a Uruguayan software engineer to work for an Indian company in Brazil? If you don't know, you risk losing the race for talent in emerging markets. These new markets are growing so fast, even established global players aren't recruiting and retaining enough employees.

How to win this contest? Ready, Hill, and Conger suggest two strategies:

- Attract talent by *making* compelling promises. Center these promises on your company's *brand* (does it have a reputation for excellence that may lead to personal advancement?), *opportunity* (will you provide challenging work, training, and competitive pay?), and *purpose* (does your company have a mission and values meaningful to potential new hires?).

- Retain talent by *keeping* your promises. Craft a culture characterized by authenticity, a merit-centered reward system, and accelerated professional development for even the lowest-level employees.

By applying these strategies, Standard Chartered Bank reduced attrition rates in its China operations by 3% over 2007–2008—while rivals suffered a dramatic *increase* in attrition.

work, stretch assignments, continual training and development, and competitive pay. In emerging markets, however, opportunity must imply an accelerated career track to senior positions. High-potential employees don't focus exclusively on climbing the ladder, however; they are willing to make lateral moves as long as their skills and experience accrue at a pace that matches the growth in their markets.

As for *purpose,* emerging-market job candidates prize a company with a game-changing business model, where they can be part of redefining their nation and the world economy. They are also attracted by a mission

Idea in Practice

Attract Talent by Making Compelling Promises

Make promises about your company's brand, opportunity, and purpose that appeal to employees in developing nations.

> *Example:* TCS Iberoamerica (a unit of Tata Consultancy Services) provides software and technology services to clients in Latin America, Spain, and Portugal, while also contributing to other TCS endeavors worldwide.

The Tata *brand* stands for technical excellence. So, when expanding into Brazil and Uruguay, TCS Iberoamerica hired local engineers (not salespeople) and sent them to India to observe its core strengths and standards. They returned home energized and eager to recruit their compatriots.

The company also promised *opportunity.* For instance, it hired local Brazilian and Uruguayan leaders who were admired in the community to head up operations—not Indian expatriates.

Finally, Tata offered an exciting *purpose*—including making a $2,000 car that would open up the industry to low-income consumers.

Retain Talent by Keeping Your Promises

It's tempting to overpromise just to get new hires in the door. But failure to deliver on those promises will sour current employees on the company and ultimately hurt its appeal for potential new hires. Keeping your promises is especially crucial in emerging markets where employees can easily move to global or local

that focuses on helping the unfortunate—many have experienced poverty firsthand—and expresses the value of global citizenship.

A company's *culture* matters in several distinct ways in emerging markets. First, its "story," or brand promise, has to feel authentic. Second, employees must be companies that seem to offer greater overall rewards.

Your company's culture plays a central role in keeping promises and retaining talent.

> *Example:* At Standard Chartered Bank's China operation, many new employees are "raw talent"—they have great potential, but lack experience. To back up its promises, the bank pays careful attention to its culture:

- **Induction.** SCB offers an intensive induction program that teaches raw-talent hires about the ethical management of financial services, including money-laundering prevention.
- **Technical training.** Relationship managers in SCB's wholesale business must complete a five-day "boot camp" and pass a strict exam before they're exposed to customers.
- **Professional and management development.** Raw recruits get intensive training in the English language, communication and listening skills, and business etiquette. They also receive career guidance and access to networking sessions.
- **Stretch assignments and deployment.** SCB's recruiting slogan "Go places" tells people that if they do well, they'll move ahead in their careers. And talented Chinese employees are often moved elsewhere, including to the group head office in London.

rewarded for reasons of merit; a high potential from Brazil or Dubai must believe that the executive suite in China or the United Kingdom is within reach. Third, although employees want to be recognized for individual achievements, they also want to feel a connection with their teams. Finally, the culture has to be truly

A framework for attracting and retaining talent

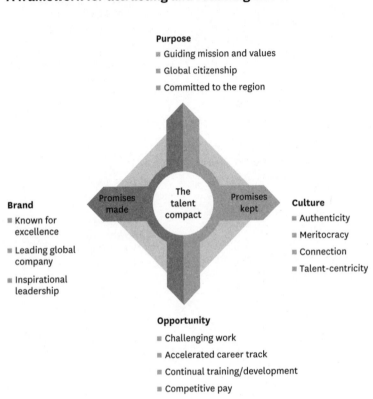

Purpose
- Guiding mission and values
- Global citizenship
- Committed to the region

Brand
- Known for excellence
- Leading global company
- Inspirational leadership

Promises made

The talent compact

Promises kept

Culture
- Authenticity
- Meritocracy
- Connection
- Talent-centricity

Opportunity
- Challenging work
- Accelerated career track
- Continual training/development
- Competitive pay

"talent-centric," so that people know they're critical to the company's success.

A closer look at our interviews gave us new insights into how these four factors work in concert. We found that they could be united under two guiding principles: *promises made* (the combination of brand, opportunity, and purpose) and *promises kept* (most significantly,

The talent market in BRIC

Although the talent gap between supply and demand is pervasive in the developing world, the particulars vary by country. The charts below show where deficits and surpluses exist in Brazil, Russia, India, and China at four levels: entry, middle management, country leadership, and regional leadership. The shaded areas represent the talent pool; the white areas show deficits or surpluses of talent. The charts illustrate averages for these countries; further analysis reveals variations across business sectors. A few highlights are boxed below.

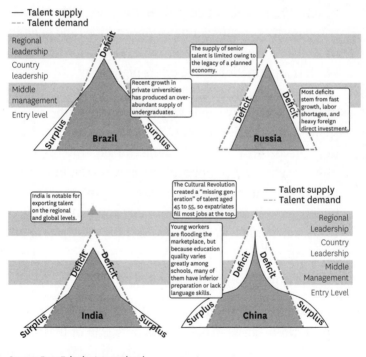

Source: Egon Zehnder International.

employees' day-to-day experiences within an organization's culture). All four factors play a role in all aspects of the talent management process, but each influences recruitment and retention in different ways. (See the exhibit "A Framework for Attracting and Retaining Talent.") Promises made and kept affect any quest for talent, but the intensity of competition in the fast-growing BRIC and other economies makes strong differentiation urgent. Most companies continue to believe that a big salary and a name brand will suffice to meet their needs, but a local company that creates genuine opportunities and exhibits desirable cultural conditions will often win out over a Western multinational that offers higher pay.

We're not proposing a simple solution to a complex problem. Company needs vary by market (see the exhibit "The Talent Market in BRIC"). Prospective employees don't necessarily value the same things: Among certain demographic groups opportunity may matter more than purpose, for instance, and individual preferences vary widely as well. But regardless of any company's strategy for a given market, the same overarching principles apply.

Attracting Talent: Promises Made

Lenovo is a good illustration of the strong lure of brand, opportunity, and purpose. Its acquisition of IBM's personal computer operations, in 2005, made it the third-largest personal computer company in the world. In 1994 the founder of Legend (as Lenovo was then known), Liu Chuanzhi, forecast that it would be a great company—an astonishing leap of faith in the early 1990s. "At the time, there were very few great Chinese companies, so Chuanzhi's vision stood out," Chen Shaopeng, president of Lenovo Greater China and senior vice president of Lenovo Group, told us. "In China, the biggest draw is Lenovo's ambition and vision." The IBM acquisition produced something of a halo effect for Lenovo, and Chinese workers felt pride that China had been able to buy part of an American business icon. Lenovo's brand was and is attractive to ambitious young workers with dreams of their own—people who are building careers and not simply looking for jobs. Lenovo was an early standout for these rising stars.

Lenovo also built a global perspective into its brand promise; to become a great company it would have to expand beyond its home market. That meant opportunity. President and CEO Bill Amelio describes his company as a "stage without a ceiling for every employee"—worldwide. In a truly global spirit, Lenovo's top-team meetings rotate among Beijing, Hong Kong, Singapore, Paris, and Raleigh, North Carolina. "Instead of having everyone travel to me, I travel to them," Amelio says. Lenovo's brand promise credibly communicates that nationality doesn't matter; if an employee demonstrates capability and vision, there are no limits. The playing field is level.

TCS Iberoamerica, a $160 million unit of Tata Consultancy Services (itself a division of the $28.5 billion Tata Group), provides software and technology services to clients in Latin America, Spain, and Portugal, while also contributing to other TCS endeavors worldwide. It's easy to understand why an Indian would want to work for Tata Group in India. But what motivates a Uruguayan software engineer to work for an Indian company in Brazil? The combination of a strong brand and opportunity. TCS Iberoamerica's president, Gabriel Rozman, told us, "When people in our region read about Tata buying Jaguar or making a $2,000 car that will change the industry . . . they get excited."

The Tata brand stands for technical excellence, so when expanding into Brazil and Uruguay, Rozman started by hiring engineers—not salespeople—and sent them to India to observe firsthand the company's core strengths and standards. They returned energized and eager to recruit their compatriots. One Uruguayan engineer saw working at Tata as an opportunity to help his country make its mark; he said, "I wanted to work at TCS because I wanted to show the world what Uruguay was all about. Even though we're a tiny country, we have value to add." Rozman also emphasized the appeal of having local Brazilian and Uruguayan leaders who are well connected and admired in the community heading up operations, rather than expatriates.

Many other managers spoke of the pride they felt in working for companies with strong brands that were also contributing to their countries' economic development. Novartis's sense of purpose, for instance, is a major draw for talent. Its Project Arogya, one of Novartis's socially conscious business operations, provides services to some 10 million villagers in 24 territories of India. Arogya's leader, Olivier Jarry, joined because of the brand promise to make lives better around the world. "We improve the health and health education of the villagers," he says.

"We provide a source of revenue for local talent working with us on the ground. We are helping local doctors and pharmacists. This is a tremendously exciting mission."

How do brand, opportunity, and purpose come together as a promise made at Standard Chartered Bank? The company's CEO, Peter Sands, explains, "We are serious about being a force for good in the world. It's not an add-on for us. We are leaders in microfinance, supporting fledgling entrepreneurs in some of the world's poorest regions. We seek out, as a part of our strategic intent, opportunities to support renewable-energy businesses. By design we are among the world's most diverse organizations, so top talents from all walks of life are attracted to us because they know they will be embraced as central to our mission, not peripheral."

Retaining Talent: Promises Kept

Brand, opportunity, and purpose can create compelling promises, but in such a competitive market the temptation is to overpromise just to get people in the door. Failure to deliver will sour current employees on the company and ultimately hurt its appeal for potential employees. That is why keeping promises—important in any market—takes on particular urgency in emerging markets, where employees can quickly and easily move to global competitors or local companies that appear to offer greater overall rewards. Many companies we've studied have experienced extraordinarily high attrition rates.

Culture, however, can play a central role in employee retention. Hemant Mishr's team at SCB sells into several of the most economically depressed areas in the world; Mishr joined SCB largely because of its brand and its purpose, which includes a commitment to supporting local communities. He stays, he says, because of the culture: SCB is a meritocracy that carefully nurtures his career, and it lives up to the values that attracted him in the first place. "It's not about pay," he says. "I could go elsewhere and earn more—lots more."

Like Mishr, many of the people we interviewed were seeking a culture that would support the promise of an accelerated career path with growth opportunities for everyone, a commitment to meritocracy, and custom career planning. HCL Technologies has such a culture. A global IT company headquartered in India, HCL employs about 55,000 people in 18 countries. When Vineet Nayar became its president, in 2005, he knew he had to do something drastic to turn around the company, formerly one of India's most innovative, which in 1999 had been first in the country in terms of revenues but by 2005 was fifth.

Nayar started with culture. He told us, "I wanted to create an environment where employee development and empowerment was the most important thing, because ultimately I wanted value-focused employees who were willing and able to drive an innovative, sophisticated experience for customers." Nayar quickly assembled a 20-person team of "young sparks," an energetic group from among HCL's top employees; they coined the slogan that became HCL's strategy for the next two years: "Employee first, customer second." The notion is simple—the best way to bring value to customers is to empower employees.

Throughout 2005 Nayar and the young sparks unveiled initiatives designed to remove barriers to employees' doing their best work. They started by revamping the company's intranet. Using a software application, employees can "raise tickets" to report problems with HCL services and processes. In real time they can watch the actions taken to correct a problem, and a ticket can be closed only by the employee who raised it. By 2006, employees were raising 30,000 tickets a month. The site also created transparency: An employee can pose any question at all to Nayar, who personally answers up to 100 inquiries a week. Shortly after its revitalization the intranet was being visited by close to 25,000 employees every week.

In addition, after a few months in office Nayar posted his own 360-degree feedback on the intranet and encouraged his senior managers to do the same; today more than 2,000 managers publicly post their feedback. Indian companies traditionally control information at the top, so the move to public 360s truly distinguished HCL. In interview after interview employees told us of the tremendous impact such transparency has on their career choices.

In another differentiating move, HCL instituted "trust pay." Many IT companies in India offer employees a combination of 70% fixed pay and 30% variable pay. In practice, high internal targets make it difficult to earn that 30%. HCL decided to offer 85% of its employees (mostly junior engineers) a fixed compensation rate, to be set at the beginning of each annual cycle. Some new hires actually thought a mistake had been made in their offer letters, because they'd never known another company to offer trust pay. This is very appealing to recruits from the developing world, because often their whole families are invested in their success. Parents, siblings, and other relatives have worked hard to send them to school, and once they know they can support their loved ones, they can focus on their work.

Because HCL has stayed true to its promises, its employees are dedicated and its customers are taking note. The company's reputation for customer service has consistently improved over the past four years, resulting in major new contracts. Nayar, who is now the CEO, says, "Putting employees first isn't about launching a few initiatives that make them feel good. It's about offering a workplace where employees, no matter their level, can have an impact, can be a part of something exciting, and can grow professionally and personally."

Leadership development is another cultural element that strongly influences retention. Careers must be carefully nurtured, and finding the time to do that may seem like a luxury when the pressure to grow is so great. But companies can't set such concerns aside, lest they lose high-potential talent as fast as they bring it in.

Lenovo very methodically provides accelerated development opportunities for its employees. Mary Eckenrod, the head of talent management, has conducted extensive research into how leaders learn and the potential career stages at technology-based organizations in emerging markets. She has worked with

Lenovo's top team to construct career maps and pipelines for every member of the company's pool of high potentials, including the CEO. All employees are asked to reflect on their career aspirations, the experiences and education that have led to their current roles in the organization, and the development they need to reach their goals.

What makes Lenovo's talent-tracking process work, however, is that the career maps are linked to key slots across the globe and accountability for the entire process rests squarely with line leadership, not with HR. Its employees are ambitious, and Lenovo needs to demonstrate that it is serious about developing their careers.

Do SCB, HCL, and Lenovo have a choice about how they approach development? Absolutely. They could focus on attracting the small handful of people with proven experience, as many companies do, but instead they hire largely on the basis of potential. They could enroll in the "cream rises to the top" school of leadership development, believing that the best talent will emerge even if the company fails to provide development opportunities. But the companies that are winning the talent race in emerging markets are not only using brand, opportunity, and purpose to attract the best people; they are investing heavily in career planning and professional development even at the lowest levels, because the workforce is so young. These companies' cultures send a powerful message to employees: Your potential is limited only by your dedication, effort, and ability to produce results.

The Talent Compact at Standard Chartered Bank

As China's economy continues to grow at a breakneck pace, thousands of new businesses are starting up, discretionary income is growing rapidly with the emergence of a new middle class, and wealth is being created as never before. Trying to recruit and retain high-caliber talent in the financial services field, the engine of much of the economy's growth, can be daunting—especially since April 2007, when the Chinese government loosened restrictions on foreign ownership of local banks. Multinational financial services firms have since flooded China.

The gap between employee supply and demand is especially wide when it comes to candidates capable of moving into senior leadership roles. Many recruits fresh out of universities lack the language and other skills to take on even entry-level positions in global companies. Nevertheless, salaries in China have risen out of proportion to the expertise of the talent pool, creating unrealistic expectations among potential employees. Moreover, China's one-child policy has created a unique problem. As one manager put it, "Consider that millions of young Chinese have no siblings and no cousins. It's not too difficult to see how the child can become the center of attention for the entire family. It's not easy giving critical feedback to someone who is not used to it and who has lots of employment options elsewhere."

Recall SCB's former difficulty in recruiting leaders for its banking operations in China. The company's strategy illustrates our framework in particularly illuminating ways.

Katherine Tsang, the CEO of SCB China since 2005, says, "These challenges forced us to tell the SCB story with passion, but to make sure that our culture and management practices matched that story in an honest way. We tell lots of stories here about our mission, our sense of purpose, and our brand, and the many opportunities that young people will get when they come to work for us. But we need to keep those promises." Together with Geraldine Haley, SCB's group head of talent management, Tsang created what the company calls the "raw talent superhighway" for SCB China, which is designed to attract and retain good people. The bank emphasizes acquiring specialized skills, followed by broad managerial training and development, followed by global networks and leadership development. Several components went into the highway's construction.

Selection

Tsang's and Haley's teams conducted extensive analyses of the skills and talents required by both retail and commercial bankers in China. Then they investigated nonbanking industries, such as travel and tourism, that had developed similar expertise, especially in customer relations. SCB China set out to aggressively recruit promising employees from these other industries; it was able to offer higher pay and significantly greater opportunities for career advancement.

Induction and Orientation

SCB runs a standard induction program, but it offers an intensive version for its raw-talent hires—employees who demonstrate the desired behaviors and values but have no skills in financial services. This program introduces recruits to the company's culture and values and teaches them the ethical management of financial services, including money-laundering prevention and codes of conduct.

Technical Training

SCB's retail division offers extensive training, and relationship managers in its wholesale business must complete a rigorous five-day "boot camp." All trainees must pass a strict examination before they are exposed to the bank's customers and clients. Skilled and seasoned managers conduct most of these sessions.

Professional and Management Development

SCB's raw recruits also get intensive training in the English language, communication and listening skills, and business etiquette, and they have a variety of ongoing educational opportunities. They receive career guidance and access to networking sessions, enabling them to explore different paths at the bank. In addition, SCB offers the Great Manager Program, which has won best-practice awards in China and elsewhere in Asia for its creativity and effectiveness in management development. The company has regional learning centers throughout China and e-learning platforms, so development is accessible to all. SCB is forming strategic partnerships with Chinese universities, both to strengthen relationships for recruitment and to offer those who join the company ongoing professional development at those schools.

Stretch Assignments and Deployment

One SCB message to recruits is captured in "Go places . . .," which has a double meaning: It tells people that if they join the bank and do well they will move ahead in their careers, and it reminds them that SCB is a global company with opportunities around the world. Chinese talent is often moved elsewhere, including to the group head office in London.

Personal Development and Performance Management

SCB employees explore their passions and strengths, with coaching and guidance, to find a starting point for their careers. Although the SCB environment is nurturing, Tsang and other leaders don't hesitate to give regular and often tough feedback. "We deal with problems openly and honestly, and that has led to the creation of an authentic and trust-based culture. People know we are a straight meritocracy, and that motivates them."

CEO Peter Sands says, "We have an exciting growth story, but more important, people can translate that story into growth opportunities for themselves. We have 25-year-olds looking at 32-year-olds doing big jobs. These young people see who they can become, and that they don't have to wait 30 years to do it." Through these efforts the bank was able to decrease attrition by 3% from 2007 to 2008. That may not sound like much, but consider that SCB is bringing thousands of people on board every year. What's more, most companies in these markets are experiencing a dramatic increase in attrition.

Thoughtful Execution

We have described principles that any company, in any market, would probably do well to heed. But emerging markets pose some special challenges worth noting. First, beware of exporting your domestic talent strategy to emerging markets. Even if that strategy is highly successful at home, it will probably need extensive tailoring to succeed in the developing world. Second, it's critical to establish a core of local talent (or of outsiders with a long history in emerging markets) that can guide you in understanding the region. Sending in a talent officer from the corporate center is unlikely to do the trick; despite the pressure to bring people on board quickly, investments in talent take root only with patience. Third, keep in mind that an overreliance on English as the "official language" of the business may prove an impediment to spotting talent. Some of your most promising people may not speak English fluently.

Finally, it's not easy to embrace and leverage diversity; companies struggle with this in the developed world, too, and very few demonstrate much diversity at the top. In emerging economies, companies have no choice but to nurture local talent, because that's the pool available and because those bright young recruits want to see others like them in positions of power. A truly merit-based company will stand out to them—particularly in hierarchical societies where getting ahead has often relied on family connections and other relationships, social status, age, or length of tenure.

People in different cultures want and expect different things from their work. Gabriel Rozman, of TCS Iberoamerica, reminded us that leading a team in India is not the same as leading a team in Brazil or Uruguay. He recognizes that his company must develop people who can lead diverse teams in various settings. Of course, this makes a commitment to keeping promises made all the more daunting, because companies can't implement one-size-fits-all processes. First figuring out which aspects of the strategy can be standardized and executed at scale and which must be sharply tuned to local needs and then coordinating implementation takes some effort—but it delivers payback. Over time, global companies may even be able to bring home some lessons about meritocracy and diversity.

As global companies are well aware, winning the race for talent in emerging markets is hard work. It requires both the explosiveness of the sprinter and the determination of the marathon runner. The framework we have outlined here should help companies assemble the workforce they need to compete on a world-class level.

DOUGLAS A. READY is a visiting professor of organizational behavior at London Business School. **LINDA A. HILL** is the Wallace Brett Donham Professor of Business Administration at Harvard Business School. **JAY A. CONGER** is the Henry R. Kravis Research Professor in Leadership Studies at Claremont McKenna College in California.

Originally published in November 2008. Reprint R0811C

What It Means to Work Here

by Tamara J. Erickson and Lynda Gratton

IT'S THE HR EQUIVALENT OF keeping up with the Joneses: In their quest to find and retain top talent, businesses often try to match competitors' offers, ensuring that their compensation schemes, health care benefits, training programs, and other talent-management practices are in line with the rest of the industry's. While this strategy may be useful for bringing job candidates to the door, it's not necessarily the most effective way to usher the right people across the threshold—great employees who will be enthusiastic about their work and fiercely loyal to the organization and its mission.

Nor does marching in lockstep with industry standards prompt companies to consider what's unique about their histories and values or potential employees' attitudes about work. Certainly, reasonable pay and a breadth of health care options matter to prospective hires, as do the tasks they'll have to perform. But people also choose jobs—and, more important, become engaged with their work—on the basis of how well their preferences and aspirations mesh with those of the organization.

Imagine yours is one of three job offers a talented candidate is mulling over. She hears a little about the orientation program at each firm. At your company, the first three months are probationary: As a new hire, the candidate would work closely with an assigned team, and when 90 days are up, the team members would vote on whether she stays or goes. Management won't have the final say. At the second company, the candidate would work on a series of fast-paced, creative projects during her first three months, under the close scrutiny of senior management. At the end of that period, she'd be expected to find a project that matched her skills. In the third company, the new hire would undergo intensive training during the first three months, learning the organization's well-defined ways of doing business; after that, she would apprentice for an extended period with one of the firm's strongest performers.

None of these orientation experiences is inherently better than the others; the prospect will pick the company whose entry program most closely reflects her own values and preferences. If she loves risk and can put up with ambiguity, she might relish the challenges and the pace of the second company but would probably be miserable with the constraints of the third. If she enjoys collaborative work, she might gravitate toward your company.

These examples underscore the importance of employee preferences in the war for talent. Unfortunately,

Idea in Brief

What separates great companies from merely good ones? Exceptional firms attract and retain the right people—employees who are excited by the company's culture and values and who reward the organization with loyalty and stellar performance.

How to get the right people on board? Don't try to be all things to all employees, Erickson and Gratton advise. Instead, communicate your company's **signature experience**—the distinctive practice that best conveys what it's *really* like to work at your company and what makes your firm unique.

Consider Whole Foods Market's signature experience: team-based hiring. Employees in each department in every store vote on whether a new hire stays or goes after a four-week trial period. This experience sends a strong message about the company's core values of collaboration and decentralization. It weeds out lone wolves—and attracts only people who share those values. Whole Foods' reward? Highly engaged and productive workers in *every* team.

they are often overlooked. What truly makes good companies great is their ability to attract and retain the right people—employees who are excited by what they're doing and the environment they're operating in. Such people are more likely to be deeply engaged in their work and less likely to chase after slightly better salaries or benefits. They will find ways to satisfy their own preferences and aspirations while meeting the organization's need to come up with creative and productive solutions to business problems. Their commitment becomes contagious, infecting customers and prospective employees. Indeed, engaged employees are the antithesis of hired guns rotating in and out of critical roles— they're productive for the long term.

Idea in Practice

To establish and leverage *your* company's signature experience, Erickson and Gratton offer these guidelines.

Define Your Target Employees

Identify your target potential employees as methodically as you do customers.

> *Example:* Unable to pay reservation agents standard industry salaries, JetBlue targeted people who prize flexible schedules. It created a signature experience reservation system: Agents work out of their homes and trade shifts using an online community board. Their job satisfaction has engendered a 30% boost in agent productivity and 38% jump in customer-service levels compared to industry averages.

Address Business Needs

Craft a signature experience that meets a specific business challenge.

> *Example:* To help integrate five recently acquired oil companies, BP developed a signature experience called "peer assist": unit heads assigned to peer groups exchange ideas about what is and isn't working in their businesses. The experience has enabled BP to meet financial and safety targets while weeding out managers who can't buy into its signature experience.

Share Your Stories

Encourage employees to relate legendary, signature experiences to potential hires.

> *Example:* One legend any MBA student worldwide is

You won't find and keep such individuals simply by aping other companies' best practices or talent-management moves, however. You need to be able to tell new and prospective hires what it's like to work at your company, to articulate the values and attributes that make working at your firm unique. You need to provide a "signature experience" that tells the right story about your company. In the process, you'll empower the people likely to hear is that of Goldman Sachs's signature recruitment experience. Successive cohorts of B-school students pass along the tale of the MBA student who went through 60 interviews before being hired. Job candidates who enjoy meeting partners in the myriad interview sessions are exactly those who will be capable of building the networks and collaborative relationships upon which the firm's success depends.

Strive for Consistency

Buttress your signature experience with processes that send consistent messages to employees.

Example: Whole Foods backs up its team-based induction process with compensation practices, employee rewards and recognition, and promotion criteria that are also strongly team based. Bonus pay, for instance, is explicitly linked to group, not individual, performance. Result? Team members choose their trainees carefully: They want hard workers, not buddies.

Have the Courage of Your Convictions

Accept that you don't need to be—nor should you try to be—all things to all people. No matter the content of your signature experience, you can use it to attract people who are suited to *your* organization's culture—and who want to further its goals.

who share your values and enthusiasm for work to self-select into your firm, thereby creating the foundation for highly productive employee-employer relationships.

Bringing Distinctiveness to Life

A signature experience is a visible, distinctive element of an organization's overall employee experience. In and of itself, it creates value for the firm, but it also serves as a powerful and constant symbol of the organization's culture and values. The experience is created by a bundle of everyday routines, or signature processes, which are tricky for competitors to imitate precisely because they have evolved in-house and reflect the company's heritage and the leadership team's ethos.

The concept of signature experiences grew out of organizational research we've conducted during the past five years. Initially, we looked closely at companies with highly engaged employees (as measured by workplace surveys and other tools) and set out to compile a checklist of the common practices these businesses used to foster enthusiastic, committed, mission-aware employees at all levels. Surprisingly, their approaches to talent management varied greatly. For instance, some firms paid well above the mean while others paid below it. Some boasted highly flexible, self-scheduling work groups; others featured more structured, "all hands on deck" environments. The companies' underlying philosophies about the employer-employee relationship also varied, from paternalistic to hands-off.

The more we looked, the more we realized that the variation in practices was not just noise in the system; it was, in fact, a critical element of the companies' ability to achieve high levels of employee engagement. These organizations excel at expressing what makes them unique. They know what they are, and it's not all things to all people. They understand their current and future employees as clearly as most companies understand their current and future customers. They recognize that individuals work for different reasons and accomplish tasks in different ways. And they demonstrate what they are vividly, with stories of actual practices and events, not through slogans on the wall or laminated values cards on every desk. As a consequence, these companies hire people who easily and enthusiastically fit in, and thereby cultivate a more committed workforce. To understand how these companies attract, engage, and retain the right kind of talent, let's take a closer look at the three signature orientation experiences we described earlier.

Whole Foods Market
The first signature experience—team-based hiring—is similar to the orientation experience at Austin, Texas–based Whole Foods Market. Potential hires are informed that each department in each store (meat, vegetables, bakery, and so on) comprises a small, decentralized entrepreneurial team whose members have complete control over who joins the group. After a four-week trial period, team members vote on whether a new hire stays or goes; the trainee needs two-thirds of the team's support in order to join the staff permanently. This signature experience is in line with Whole Foods' profit-sharing program. Thirteen times a year, the company calculates the performance of each team. Members of the teams that do well receive up to $2 per hour extra in their paychecks. That bonus pay is explicitly linked to group rather than individual performance, so team members choose their trainees carefully—they want workers, not buddies. This entry into the company undoubtedly weeds out lone

wolves and conveys a strong message about the firm's core values of collaboration and decentralization. This signature experience seems to be working: Whole Foods has appeared on *Fortune*'s list of the 100 Best Companies to Work For nine years in a row.

Trilogy Software

The second orientation experience described earlier—trial under fire—is patterned after the signature experience at Trilogy Software, a rapidly growing software and services provider also based in Austin, Texas. New employees go through an exhausting three-month immersion process, a sort of organizational boot camp, in which top management, including the CEO, oversees their every step. In the first month, new recruits participate in fast-paced creative projects, in teams of about 20, under the mentorship of more-experienced colleagues called section leaders. In the second month, the project teams are shuffled and split into smaller "breakthrough teams" charged with inventing product or service ideas, creating business models, building prototypes, and developing marketing plans—all in hyperaccelerated fashion. In the third month, the recruits have to demonstrate their capacity for personal initiative. Some continue working on their breakthrough teams; others find sponsors elsewhere in the company and work on their projects. Upon completion of the program, candidates undergo rigorous evaluation and receive detailed feedback on their performance from colleagues, section leaders, and senior management. The new hires are sent to different parts of the organization, but the bonds they develop during this extreme orientation period remain strong throughout their careers.

Trilogy's signature orientation experience serves as the company's primary R&D engine: Recruits' projects have produced more than $25 million direct revenues and have formed the basis for more than $100 million in new business. The experience also serves as a proving ground for Trilogy's next generation of leaders: the mentors and coaches who guide the members of the breakthrough teams as well as the new hires themselves. Most important, Trilogy's orientation experience provides a compelling illustration of life in the firm. A candidate who prefers a clear-cut, well-defined work environment will almost certainly decline after hearing the details of the immersion process. But a candidate who likes intense challenges and can tolerate some ambiguity early on will probably jump right in.

The Container Store

The third orientation experience—extensive training and indoctrination in a proven approach—is from the Container Store, a Dallas-based retailer of storage solutions ranging from the basic (Tupperware) to the sophisticated (customized shelving systems). Some of its products are quite expensive—a single custom-designed closet system, for instance, may cost several thousand dollars—so the floor staff's ability to meet customers' expectations can have huge financial implications. Because the company depends on employees to be capable of suggesting storage options that will match a customer's requirements, its induction process consists of immediate and intense training. All new hires in the stores, distribution centers, and headquarters (full-time and seasonal employees) go through Foundation Week—five days dedicated to absorbing information about the Container Store's products, processes, and values, plus extracurricular HR paperwork and reading. New employees assume regular work schedules only after having completed the five full days of training—and even then they usually apprentice for a while with some of the company's star performers. The employee education doesn't stop there: In their first year at the Container Store, all staffers receive at least 235 hours of formal training, compared with an average of about seven hours in the retail industry overall. Employees spend time in different functions and units to gain a broader perspective and to learn about the company's strategic challenges.

The Container Store's signature experience sends the right messages about employee fit and long-term opportunities: More than 40% of new employees are recommended by friends who work for the company. Employee surveys reveal that, on average, 97% of them agree with the statement, "People care about each other here." And employee turnover is less than 30%, significantly lower than the industry average. Obviously, some job applicants will be impressed with the clarity and rigor of the Container Store's commitment to training; others won't. But a hiring manager's description of this intense orientation experience certainly sends a clear signal to a potential employee about what it takes to succeed at the company.

By defining and communicating their core values and distinctive attributes in unique and memorable ways, Whole Foods Market, Trilogy Software, and the Container Store empower potential hires to make well-informed employment choices. These companies likewise are increasing the probability that they're bringing aboard highly engaged and highly motivated workers.

Finding Your Signature

Companies that successfully create and communicate signature experiences understand that different types of people will excel at different companies, and that not all workers want the same things. In a series of studies conducted jointly with researchers Ken Dychtwald and Bob Morison, Tamara Erickson categorized workers into six segments on the basis of why and how they like to work. Some care deeply about the social connections and friendships formed in the workplace, for instance. Others just want to make as much money with as much flexibility and as little commitment as possible. Some have an appetite for risk. Others crave the steadiness of a well-structured, long-term climb up the career ladder. (See the exhibit, "A Job by Any Other Name.")

The firms we've studied that have engendered highly productive, highly engaged workforces acknowledge and address these differences more effectively than their competitors. Specifically, they follow some general

A job by any other name

As many societies become increasingly affluent, more and more people have the luxury of allowing work to fill a variety of roles in their lives. Studies conducted by Tamara Erickson and researchers Ken Dychtwald and Bob Morison suggest that work plays six general roles, which correspond to six types of employees, based on psychodemographic characteristics. Each worker segment cares deeply about several aspects of the employee-employer relationship and little about the others.

Employee type	Expressive legacy	Secure progress	Individual expertise and team success	Risk and reward	Flexible support	Low obligation and easy income
The role of work	*Work is about creating something with lasting value.*	*Work is about improving one's lot in life and finding a predictable path.*	*Work is about being a valuable part of a winning team.*	*Work is one of multiple opportunities to live a life filled with change and excitement.*	*Work is a source of livelihood but not yet (or not currently) a priority.*	*Work is a source of immediate economic gain.*
What appeals and engages	Autonomy Entrepreneurial opportunities Creative opportunities	Fair, predictable rewards Concrete compensation, solid benefits and retirement package	Collaboration Fun	Opportunity to improve personal finances Flexibility	Flexibility Well-defined vacation and family benefits	Jobs that are relatively easy to come by Well-defined work routines

Stimulating tasks that enable continual learning and growth	Stability	Stability and structure	Opportunity to choose tasks and positions from a long menu of options	Well-defined work routines—the ability to plug in and out of tasks and assignments with ease	Lucrative compensation and benefits packages
	Structure and routine	Opportunity to gain competence	Open-ended tasks and approaches to getting work done	Virtual, asynchronous tasks and assignments	Stability and security
	Career training	Opportunity to leverage personal strengths		Fun	Recognition

Source: A statistical survey of the U.S. workforce conducted jointly by the Concours Institute and Age Wave, a research and communications company, and funded by 24 major corporations.

principles for creating, supporting, and preserving their unique employee experiences:

Target a Segment of Potential Employees

Most executives can tell you which consumers will buy their products or services. Few have the same insight into which job candidates will buy into the organization's culture and adapt to its workflow. Companies that target potential employees as methodically as they do potential customers can gain a sustainable market advantage. That's been the case at JetBlue. Since its launch in 1999, the airline has defied many common industry practices, including the traditional approach to flight reservations. When most airlines were using standard call centers, JetBlue devised a system based entirely out of employees' homes. This has become one of the airline's signature experiences and part of its organizational lore, attracting a strong and productive base of employees who find flexible schedules more valuable than above-average compensation.

According to founder and CEO David Neeleman, it was more than cost savings that prompted the company to create this signature experience. Like the flight crew, the reservations agents are the face of JetBlue, responsible for ensuring high levels of customer satisfaction that will translate into increased revenues. The company couldn't afford to pay the agents huge salaries, however, so senior management decided to appeal to them in a different way—by letting them work from their homes. "We train them, send them home, and they are happy," Neeleman says.

JetBlue tries to accommodate call center agents' varied scheduling requirements—some may work only 20 hours a week, for instance, or may need to swap shifts at the last minute—but the airline balances those preferences against its business objectives. Employees have unlimited shift-trading privileges, which they can negotiate using an online community board. This self-scheduling process keeps employees motivated and satisfied, which means they're more likely to provide better customer care. For its part, JetBlue has enjoyed a 30% boost in agent productivity, a 38% increase in customer-service levels, and a 50% decrease in management workload per agent, compared with industry norms.

Bright Horizons, a leading provider of employer-sponsored child care, has crafted a signature experience that also begins with the reconceptualization of a critical organizational role—that of the classroom teachers in its centers. These individuals are never referred to by common terms such as "child care worker" or "babysitter." Instead, Bright Horizons hires "early childhood educators" for its classrooms, thereby attracting people who see themselves as long-term professionals in a field full of temp workers. This important shift sets the stage for an employee experience in line with the firm's mission statement, which, among other things, pledges to "nurture each child's unique qualities and potential" and to "create a work environment that encourages professionalism." Reinforcing this signature experience are the company's team-based approach to hiring; a welcome program that makes it clear to new hires (and their families) that they have joined an organization that is serious about excellence and professionalism; and strong skills-based training and promotion opportunities. In an industry known for high turnover—the average is about 50%—Bright Horizon's turnover runs from 20% to 22%.

Address Specific Business Needs

Some companies' signature experiences stem from critical business needs. For instance, several years ago Lord John Browne, the CEO of BP, was faced with the daunting task of bringing together five oil companies BP had recently acquired. The challenge was to create a culture of learning across the company's 120 business units; without such integration, none of the anticipated cost-benefit synergies would materialize. At the time, many of the business unit heads were adept at competing, but few were adept at collaborating. To address this gap, Browne and his colleagues developed a signature experience called "peer assist." The business unit heads are assigned to peer groups representing as many as 13 units, and the members are required to exchange ideas and information about what is and is not working in their businesses. (To encourage knowledge sharing, much of each business unit leader's bonus pay depends on the performance of the whole peer group.) Employees are learning from one another. Thanks in part to these cross-platform groups, BP has met its financial targets and talent-management criteria. The beauty of this signature experience is that it clearly demonstrates Browne's basic operational philosophy: Peers working together will be the foundation of BP's success. Managers who can't buy into the signature experience won't waste their time or the organization's.

Identify and Preserve Your History

The seed of a signature experience already exists in many companies. Their challenge is to find it, extend or shape it to the needs of today's business, and protect it. Consider Royal Bank of Scotland, which can credit its rise from a small national bank to one of the largest financial institutions in the world to a work environment that values action and speed. Those who do best in the bank deliver high-quality results quickly and under intense pressure—which is why prospects need to hear about RBS's historic signature experience.

In the eighteenth century, when the financial institution was founded, banking was a gentleman's pursuit. The day's business was usually completed by lunchtime so that businessmen could get on to more important matters in the afternoon—fishing, hunting, and the like. That schedule was made possible by the morning meeting. Now, of course, banking is a 24-hour business, and there's much less time for afternoon jaunts through the Scottish hills. But the morning meeting lives on. Successive RBS CEOs have adopted this practice and made it their own. The current executive team meets with the chief executive, Sir Fred Goodwin, every morning between 8 and 9 to talk about the previous day's events, go over that day's agenda, and plan for the future. The sessions force employees to think about speed to market; RBS talks about completing projects within 30, 60, or 90 days—there is no mention of weeks or months. The morning meetings reinforce the collective account-ability of the senior team.

RBS knows that early morning meetings and short-term, fast-paced projects won't appeal to everyone. So its signature experience sends an explicit message to potential hires: There are plenty of jobs out there for those who need a caffeine jolt and a few minutes with the *Times* before making a decision—just not at RBS.

Another firm with a signature experience rooted in its history is W.L. Gore & Associates, a private firm headquartered in Delaware. The company's best-known product, Gore-Tex, is used in clothing worn by adventurers the world over. W.L. Gore attributes its steady growth to an employee experience built around the so-called "lattice" system of management—no hier-archies, no predetermined channels of communication, and no defined jobs locking associates (they're never called employees) into particular tasks. This approach, which founder Bill Gore introduced more than 40 years ago, has been protected and reinforced ever since. As-sociates have sponsors, not bosses. They don't have jobs; they make voluntary promises to meet general ex-pectations within functional areas—running a particu-lar machine, for instance, or crunching numbers. For their part, sponsors commit to helping new associates find "quick wins"—projects that put the recruits on a fast track for success while acclimatizing them to the organization.

W.L. Gore's general processes uphold this signature ex-perience. For instance, associates are compensated on the basis of the quantity, quality, and financial outcomes of their work. Performance is reviewed twice each year, and peers and sponsors get to weigh in on their colleagues' work. They share their feedback with a compensation committee—there are about 15 such committees within the company, one for each functional area of the business—that then ranks people who handle a particular function from the highest contributor to the lowest. (The associate's rank is determined by contributions to the success of the business, not just personal achievements.) Using guidelines based on external salary data, the company pays the associates at the top of the list more than those at the bottom. The objective is to be internally fair and externally competitive.

Employees who want clear definition in their work would probably hate W.L. Gore's emphasis on personal ownership and commitment; those who are comfortable in a high-reward but somewhat uncertain environment would be likely to thrive.

Share Your Stories

One of the legends any MBA student is likely to hear is that of Goldman Sachs's signature recruitment experience. Successive cohorts of B-school students worldwide pass along the tale of the MBA student who went through 60 interviews before being hired. That story isn't an urban myth. The selection process is truly an endurance test, requiring enormous resources. In a given year, about 5,000 applicants speak to ten members of the firm, and the top 2,500 speak to more than 30. Each year, Goldman Sachs invests more than

100,000 man-hours in conversations with prospective employees.

The seemingly endless interviews are not designed to ferret out candidates' intellectual prowess or previous work experiences—that's what the GMAT scores and application forms are for. The process is a reflection of the company's deep commitment to internal collaboration and networking and serves as a preview of life in the firm. At Goldman Sachs, there is no room for individual stars. Prospective candidates who hear the stories and enjoy meeting partners in the myriad interview sessions are exactly those, the firm believes, who will be capable of building networks and strong collaborative relationships.

Employees at Starbucks have their own tales to pass on. When recruiting baristas, the company looks for people with outgoing personalities and strong social skills. To convey these attributes and prompt customer-savvy individuals to self-select into the firm, Starbucks tells all prospective hires about its mandatory in-store immersion process. Every new Starbucks employee—even at the corporate level—goes through a 24-hour paid training module called First Impressions. The standardized curriculum focuses on learning about coffee and creating a positive customer experience. This is followed by in-store training—employees spend time making beverages, talking to customers, and learning the business on the floor. Employees at all levels say this hands-on experience is essential preparation for any role within the company. And they swap stories about candidates who ditched the process early on, just because they didn't want to spend weeks working in the stores. Indeed, the satisfied lot who stuck with it and poured lattes for a while tell these tales with great pride.

Strive for Consistency

A signature experience must be buttressed by processes that send consistent messages to employees. Our research shows that one of the most common causes of low engagement in organizations is employees' perception that some elements of the work experience aren't exactly as they were advertised. How many times have we all heard people, six months into a job, say, "It's just not what I expected or wanted."

Several years ago, a large industrial company asked us to help redesign its orientation process, which executives at the firm felt was turning people off and driving them away. When we took a close look, we concluded that the orientation process wasn't the problem; it accurately reflected the highly structured, tightly managed nature of the organization. The problem was occurring much earlier, during recruitment, when the company promised prospective employees a flexible work environment full of excitement and innovation. This company was not a bad place to work, but it was doing a poor job of targeting and attracting people who would thrive there. It needed to change either the pitch it used with job candidates or the experience of working at the firm.

Whole Foods backs up its team-based induction process with compensation practices, employee rewards and recognition, and promotion criteria that are also strongly team based. All elements of the overall

Elements of Engagement

To foster deeply committed employees, you need the following:

- A comprehensive understanding of the types of people who will be productive in your organization over the long term. What kinds of skills should they have? What should be their attitudes toward work?

- A well-defined, well-communicated signature experience that conveys for potential hires and reinforces for employees the attributes and values of the organization.

- A coherent employee experience—none of your company's environmental elements misrepresents what it's really like to work there.

---

employee experience are aligned. Likewise, Goldman Sachs's commitment to cooperative networks and its "one firm" mentality are reinforced in multiple ways, including through its promotion practices. Attention is given not only to an individual's commercial acumen but also to the extent to which he or she is a culture carrier for the company. Representatives across the company, not just within specific divisions or product lines, participate in the evaluation and selection of partners.

Have the Courage of Your Convictions

Companies—even very large ones—don't need to be all things to all people. In fact, they shouldn't try to be. No matter the content of your signature experience, you can attract people who are suited to your organization's culture and interested in furthering its goals. Conversely, you must be willing to accept that your employment proposition won't appeal to everyone. Exxon Mobil, for instance, readily acknowledges that its highly structured environment isn't for everyone, and a number of employees choose to leave early in their tenures. The company's demands are exacting; employees are expected to follow clear communication protocols and strict security regulations—as you might expect in an industry in which safety is a high priority. Interestingly, however, attrition among employees who make it past the five-year mark is almost nil, and the level of engagement among them is very high. Perhaps there's a more effective way for the company to communicate the structured nature of its work experience to prospective hires, but Exxon Mobil's signature experience is strong enough and cohesive enough to retain those who are likely to be engaged and productive in the firm for the long term.

The company's executives calmly recognize their plight. "The suit was too tight," they say, as they describe those who departed early on. That statement serves as a polite but powerful reminder that Exxon Mobil's employee experience is unlikely to flex on the basis of one individual's preferences and that opting out is an acceptable path. Management understands that the company's signature experience won't necessarily map to every stage of the employee life cycle. And management carefully and sensitively protects the processes that contribute to this secure, structured experience. For example, the company recently considered switching from a defined benefits plan to a defined contribution plan, which the majority of companies today favor for their employees. In the end, it concluded that the security the defined benefits plan provides is more in sync with the values of the employees the company hopes to retain.

People will become long-term, deeply engaged employees of your company if their work experience is what they expect it to be and if your firm's values and attributes match theirs. You do a disservice to your organization—and to prospective employees—if you try to be all things to all people. The best strategy for coming out ahead in the war for talent isn't to scoop up everyone in sight, unless you want to deal with the fallout: high turnover, high recruitment and training costs, and disengaged, unproductive employees. Instead, you need to convince the right people—those who are intrigued and excited by the work environment you can realistically offer and who will reward you with their loyalty—to choose you.

TAMARA J. ERICKSON is the president of the Concours Institute, the research and education arm of the professional services firm The Concours Group. **LYNDA GRATTON** is a professor of management practice at London Business School.

Originally published in March 2007. Reprint R0703G

The Risky Business of Hiring Stars

by Boris Groysberg, Ashish Nanda, and Nitin Nohria

IF YOU'RE LIKE MOST CEOS we know, you're down in the trenches, leading your company's war for talent from the front. The battle for the best and brightest people may be less fierce than it was five years ago, but, along with the U.S. economy, it's heating up again. At any rate, you've been hiring top performers wherever you could unearth them during the recession; that's way too important to delay or delegate. And when you do stumble across first-rate talent, you're willing to offer those stellar executives almost anything to come and work for you: huge salaries, signing bonuses, stock options—whatever it takes.

After all, you're pretty certain that companies can defeat rivals in the global knowledge economy by deploying better talent at all levels. Only the pick of the class can cope with today's business world, where executives have to anticipate change, adapt quickly, and make decisions amid uncertainty, right? Besides, A players are ambitious, brainy, dynamic—and charismatic. When you recruit talent from outside the organization, which is inevitable since developing people within the firm takes time and money, why settle for B players? Hitch your wagon to a rising star, and the company's profits will soar.

That's a powerful idea, and several books and management gurus have popularized various shades of it over the past decade. In fact, it's the cornerstone of people management strategies in many companies. There's only one problem. Like many popular ideas, it doesn't work.

For all the hype that surrounds stars, human resources experts have rarely studied their performance over time. Six years ago, we started tracking high-flying CEOs, researchers, and software developers, as well as leading professionals in investment banking, advertising, public relations, management consulting, and the law. We observed that top performers in all those groups were more like comets than stars. They were blazing successes for a while but quickly faded out when they left one company for another. Since it wasn't at all clear why stars were unable to extend their achievements across companies, we decided to delve more deeply into the phenomenon.

We recently completed an in-depth study of 1,052 star stock analysts who worked for 78 investment banks in the United States from 1988 through 1996. For the

Idea in Brief

Are you hiring industry stars, no matter what the cost, to defeat rivals? If so, beware: fighting—and winning—the star wars could be the worst thing you ever do for your company.

Why? Top performers resemble comets more than stars: once they're lured to another firm, their performance plummets by as much as 20%—permanently. That's because just 30% of a star's performance stems from individual capabilities; 70% derives from resources and qualities specific to the company that developed him—such as reputation, information technologies, leadership, training, and team chemistry.

When you hire a star, he leaves all that support behind—so his performance flags. Worse, his group's performance slips, as resentment over the star's spectacular hiring package corrodes morale and productivity. Meanwhile, your company's market valuation erodes, as investors decide you overpaid to bag your star.

The lesson? Grow your stars, don't buy them. Recruit bright people through disciplined hiring strategies. Use training and mentoring to develop them. Then strive to retain them—by helping them broaden their skills, publicly recognizing them, and easing their work/life tension.

By applying this formula, investment bank Lehman Brothers kept many of its stars—despite paying them 25% to 30% less than what rival companies paid similar high performers.

study's purpose, we defined a star as any analyst who was ranked by *Institutional Investor* magazine as one of the best in the industry in any of those nine years. As the sidebar on our methodology explains (see "Methodology to Watch Stars By"), we chose to study Wall Street's jet set partly because we found data on both their performance and movements between companies. The study was limited to that one group,

Idea in Practice

To grow your own stars:

Recruit good people. Use disciplined hiring practices to attract promising candidates. In Lehman Brothers' research department, multiple interviewers looked for specific qualities in each job candidate—particularly intellectual capacity and work ethic, the ability to represent these qualities to clients orally or in writing, and likeability. Interviewers decided candidates' fate by consensus: if any interviewer had irresolvable concerns, the firm passed on the applicant.

Establish supports. Encourage high performance by creating supportive structures, such as:

- **Systems and processes.** Establish procedures and routines that fuel individuals' success.

Lehman Brothers, for instance, developed processes that help analysts evaluate research rigorously, deliver reports ahead of rivals, and keep up-to-date on their performance.

- **Leadership.** Even talented employees need coaching and mentoring to excel. When Lehman Brothers' equity research department was the best on Wall Street, its star analysts attributed their success predominantly to their bosses' nuts-and-bolts guidance.

- **Internal networks.** Encourage people to forge relationships across functions; they'll deliver better results. Investment firm Sanford C. Bernstein became renowned for its research by teaming

however, and it's necessary to be careful about over-generalizing the implications. Still, our findings were surprising, to say the least.

When a company hires a star, the star's performance plunges, there is a sharp decline in the functioning of the group or team the person works with, and the company's market value falls. Moreover, stars don't stay with organizations for long, despite the astronomical analysts with salespeople, who communicated analysts' recommendations directly to clients.

- **Training.** Offer programs that accelerate talented employees' development. In Lehman Brothers' training program, veteran analysts offered sessions on subjects like analyzing balance sheets, "creating something special in your research," and "how not to say stupid things to the press." The program not only benefited learners; it granted recognition to expert analysts and made them feel part of a fraternity.

- **Teams.** Working with smart colleagues sparks ideas that stimulate productivity. Encourage high performers' teammates to counsel and coach them. Ingrain a team mentality: legendary Goldman Sachs coleader John Whitehead once cautioned an analyst that "at Goldman Sachs, we never say 'I.'"

Use savvy retention strategies. Retaining stars requires more than salaries. Understand what motivates your high performers, then take steps to satisfy their interests. For example, investment firms Sanford C. Bernstein and Lehman Brothers, understanding their stars' need for a sense of achievement, publicly recognized high flyers' contributions. Aware that top analysts wanted to broaden their skills, both companies invited them to speak on behalf of their firms at conferences.

salaries firms pay to lure them away from rivals. For all those reasons, companies cannot gain a competitive advantage by hiring stars from outside the business. Instead, they should focus on growing talent within the organization and do everything possible to retain the stars they create. As we shall show in the following pages, companies shouldn't fight the star wars, because winning could be the worst thing that happens to them.

Methodology to Watch Stars By

WE FIRST STARTED TRACKING CORPORATE America's stars, such as CEOs of *Fortune* 100 companies, chief software developers, and ace investment bankers, as well as hotshots in advertising, consulting, and corporate law, in 1998. Stars had two characteristics: They were superior performers and they were treated as such by employers. Over the years, we started noticing that many stars didn't perform as well after they left the companies where they had earned their reputations. That's when we began to wonder if executive performance is as easily portable as employers (and employees) believe.

To analyze the performance of stars over a long period of time, we decided to focus on star stock analysts (they are also called research or sell-side analysts) in the United States. There are several reasons why we chose to focus on that competitive, high-profile, and highly paid group (star analysts earned $2 million to $5 million a year then).

First, we could get reliable data on both the performance of star stock analysts and their movements between companies. We used a reliable proxy for performance. Since 1972, *Institutional Investor* has published an annual ranking of the best stock analysts. The magazine asks institutional money managers to rank the analysts who "have been most helpful to you and your institution in researching U.S. equities over the past 12 months." The money managers evaluate analysts on six criteria: earnings estimates, accessibility and responsiveness, service quality, stock selection, industry knowledge, and written reports. They give every analyst a numerical score, and *Institutional Investor* weights the scores by the size of the voting firms. The magazine ranks the top four analysts (first, second, third, and runner-up) for every industry. The rankings are accepted both on Wall Street and by academics as a reliable proxy for analysts' performance. Several studies have shown that the forecasts made by ranked analysts are superior to those of unranked analysts. Ranked analysts generate more accurate and more frequent forecasts, and their reports have a bigger impact on stock prices. In 1996, less than 5% of all the analysts in the United States were ranked analysts, or, according to our definition, stars.

Second, we chose to focus on stock analysts because they suffer few distractions when they change companies. Most analysts live in the New York area, and when they switch jobs, they usually don't have to relocate. They don't change the sectors they track when they join other organizations, because companies hire them for their specialized knowledge. Moreover, the analysts' customers don't change, because institutional investors refer to 24 reports, on average, per industry before making decisions. It would there-fore be logical for us to attribute the change in a star analyst's per-formance mainly to the change in the organizational setting.

Third, we suspected that most companies and executives believed that the performance of research analysts, and especially that of stars, depended on their talent. For instance, 85% of the people we interviewed on Wall Street believed that the analysts' perform-ance was independent of the companies they worked for. If we were able to establish that the performance of stock analysts was not portable, it would most likely follow that performance was not portable for most other executives or professions either.

From *Institutional Investor*, we gathered data on name, industry sec-tor, type (equity versus fixed income), rank, year of ranking, and company affiliation for both equity analysts (who are ranked every October) and fixed-income analysts (who are ranked every August) from 1988 through 1996. Over that nine-year period, we found 4,200 analyst-year combinations (3,514 equity and 686 fixed-income ana-lysts). If every analyst who appeared in the rankings was counted only once, the list included 798 equity analysts and 254 fixed-income analysts and added up to 1,052 star analysts who worked for 78 investment banks. By comparing the rankings with the movements of the analysts over the years, we were able to figure out the changes in performance when they changed companies. To round off the research, we studied 24 investment banks in depth, conducting 167 hours of interviews with 86 stock analysts and their supervisors.

When Companies Hire Stars

Three things happen when a company hires a star, and none of them bodes well for the organization.

The Star's Luster Fades

The star's performance falls sharply and stays well below his old achievement levels thereafter. Our data show that 46% of the research analysts did poorly in the year after they left one company for another. After they switched loyalties, their performance plummeted by an average of about 20% and had not climbed back to the old levels even five years later. So the decline in the stars' performance was more or less permanent. There's no dearth of examples: James Cunningham, who was ranked Wall Street's top specialty chemicals analyst from 1983–1986, dropped to third place as soon as he left F. Eberstadt for First Boston. Likewise, Paul Mlotok, who specialized in tracking international oil stocks, dropped from number one in 1988 to number three the following year, when he moved from Salomon Brothers to Morgan Stanley.

Obviously, a star doesn't suddenly become less intelligent or lose a decade of work experience overnight when she switches firms. Although most companies overlook this fact, an executive's performance depends on both her personal competencies and the capabilities, such as systems and processes, of the organization she works for. When she leaves, she cannot take the firm-specific resources that contributed to her achievements.

As a result, she is unable to repeat her performance in another company; at least, not until she learns to work the new system, which could take years.

Top performers who join new companies find that the transitions they must make are tougher than they had anticipated. When a star tries to learn about the procedures, personalities, relationships, and subcultures of the organization, he is handicapped by the attitudes of his new colleagues. Resentful of the rainmaker (and his pay), other managers avoid the newcomer, cut off information to him, and refuse to cooperate. That hurts the star's ego as well as his ability to perform. Meanwhile, he has to unlearn old practices as he learns new ones. But stars are unusually slow to adopt fresh approaches to work, primarily because of their past successes, and they are unwilling to fit easily into organizations. They become more amenable to change only when they realize that their performance is slipping. By that time, they have developed reputations that are hard to change.

It isn't surprising that stars don't stay with companies for long. Around 36% of the stock analysts left the investment banks that hired them within 36 months, and another 29% quit in the next 24 months. That's a high rate of attrition even by Wall Street standards. Once stars start changing jobs, they keep moving to the highest bidders instead of allowing employers to build businesses around them. In fact, the study showed that every additional job that an analyst had held increased the probability of the individual's leaving.

The Group's Performance Slips

Most executives realize that a star's appointment will hurt the morale of the people she will work with, but they underestimate the aftershocks. The arrival of a highflier often results in interpersonal conflicts and a breakdown of communication in the group. As a result, the group's performance suffers for several years. Sometimes, the team (or what is left of it) returns to normal only after the star has left the company.

The money that stars make isn't the only problem. Their coworkers often become demotivated because they feel they must look outside the organization if they want to grow or to occupy leadership positions. Their suspicions are fueled by the fact that senior executives provide more resources to a newly hired star than to a company stalwart even if both have performed equally well. Companies are eager to please stars and often offer resources as part of the hiring package. Loyal employees become embittered, because without resources, they cannot perform as well as the hired guns. Junior managers take the star's induction as a signal that the organization isn't interested in tapping their potential. That often results in demoralization in the group.

At one investment bank, the head of the research department told us: "I painfully learned that hiring a star analyst resembles an organ transplant. First, the new body can reject the prized organ that operated so well inside another body. . . . On some occasions, the new organ hurts healthy parts of the body by demanding a disproportionate blood supply. . . . Other parts of the body start to resent it, ache, and . . . demand attention . . . or threaten to stop working. You should think about it very carefully before you do [a transplant] to a healthy body. You could get lucky, but success is rare."

The Company's Valuation Suffers

In spite of the positive publicity companies get when they sign up stars, investors perceive the appointments as value-destroying events. For example, in 1994, every hiring announcement by Bear Stearns, Merrill Lynch, and Salomon Brothers resulted in a fall in their stock prices. We found that the stock prices of the investment banks we studied fell by 0.74%, on average, and investors lost an average of $24 million each time the firms announced that they had hired a star. That's ironic, because companies usually roped in stars when their stock prices were underperforming relative to the industry.

Many investors apparently believe that while compensation for a star with long tenure is more or less commensurate with performance, rivals are blinded by stars' status and overpay in order to bag them. Second, shareholders seem to assume that most stars leave when they are near their peak and that their performance will decline after they join a new firm. Third, canny investors interpret a star's recruitment as a signal that the company has embarked on a hiring spree. For instance, one investment bank hired 20 executives within six months of recruiting a star analyst—and overpaid many of them, too. The stock market anticipates the impact of all the future hires on the company's wage bill and pulls its share price down.

Clearly, when companies try to grow by hiring stars, it doesn't work. Over the last two decades, several financial institutions have tried to break into the U.S. investment banking industry by luring away their rivals' best stock analysts. None of them made much headway, and most pulled back after losing millions in the process. For instance, in 1987, Prudential Securities kicked off Project '89, hoping to become one of the top investment banks in the United States over the ensuing four years. In the first five months, the company hired 30 senior investment bankers and 12 star analysts. Prudential offered higher salaries and bonuses than any other company on Wall Street, and unlike other firms, it didn't tie them to performance. But the company soon ran up losses and had to abandon its game plan. Not only did Prudential stop recruiting more analysts by 1988, it also fired 25% of the stars it had hired.

Similarly, when investment bank Drexel Burnham Lambert collapsed in February 1990, Arthur Kirsch, then the head of its equity operation, cherry-picked 70 professionals. They moved with him to County NatWest Securities, the U.S. securities arm of National Westminster Bank, a British bank that was trying to grow. In less than two years, most of the stars had defected because they could not rebuild their franchises. In December 1992, Kirsch too resigned, and County NatWest gave up trying to become a power player on Wall Street. Another example is Barclays de Zoete Wedd (BZW), Barclays Bank's investment banking arm, which snapped up 40 star analysts and salespeople from Drexel in 1990. Less than a year later, BZW asked

Howard Coates, the head of the firm's equities division, to step down because of the losses the operation had run up. His successor, Jonathan Davie, ended BZW's attempt to grow by collecting scalps and asked many of the expensive new recruits to leave.

The Drivers of Star Performance

Most of us have an instinctive faith in talent and genius, but it isn't just that people make organizations perform better. The organization also makes people perform better. In fact, few stars would change employers if they understood the degree to which their performance is tied to the company they work for. One indicator: When researchers studied the performance of 2,086 mutual fund managers between 1992 and 1998, they found that 30% of a fund's performance could be attributed to the individual and 70% was due to the manager's institution.[1]

Our study confirmed that company-specific competencies drive stars' performance. We drew a distinction between the six biggest investment banks (Credit Suisse First Boston, Goldman Sachs, Lehman Brothers, Merrill Lynch, Morgan Stanley, and Salomon Brothers) and the other 72 firms we studied because the first group provided employees with many more resources than the latter did. Of the analysts we studied, 57% moved between companies with similar capabilities, a quarter left one of the six biggest investment banks for one of the smaller ones, and 18% moved up from small to big. As we had suspected, the performance drop was most pronounced after the star analysts moved from one of the big companies to one of the small firms, losing company-specific resources in the process. When stars hopped between companies with similar capabilities, their performance dipped for only two years. From the third year on, they did as well as the analysts who had not changed firms, presumably because they were able to pick up some company-specific skills. The performance of analysts who migrated from smaller to bigger firms often did not dip, possibly because they acquired new resources, although they still didn't do any better than before the move. Moreover, stars who brought with them teams of research analysts, salespeople, and traders performed better than analysts who moved solo. Thus, the company is a large part of the reason why stars become and stay stars.

Everyone is familiar with the individual factors that contribute to performance: innate abilities, education (including professional training), and a person's external social networks (industry contacts and some clients). But most companies underestimate the degree to which stars' success depends on the following company-specific factors:

Resources and Capabilities

Only after a star quits does he realize that the company's reputation as well as its financial and human resources allowed him to do the things that really mattered. A star analyst who left Merrill Lynch for a smaller investment bank told us: "I spent three days trying to get the investment relations people at a company to give me some information that would have taken my assistant at Merrill less than an hour to obtain. Then I tried to populate a spreadsheet with some sector data that was available at my fingertips at Merrill but was nonexistent at the new company."

Systems and Processes

Though stars often complain about them, corporate procedures and routines contribute in many ways to individuals' success. When Lehman Brothers' research department was ranked number one in 1990, its star analysts had nothing but praise for a team-based research process that allowed them to work across sectors and an investment committee process that helped them evaluate research rigorously. They also made special mention of Lehman Brothers' information technology systems, which allowed analysts to deliver reports ahead of rivals, and an evaluation system that kept analysts up-to-date on how they were performing.

Leadership

In most companies, bosses give talented employees the resources and support they need to become stars. In the firms we studied, it was up to research directors to decide how analysts should allocate their time, what companies they should cover, how many reports they should write, and how many client visits and telephone calls they should make. The directors also determined what proportion of the departmental budget should go to each analyst and what her compensation should be. It was impossible for analysts to survive without supportive supervisors. Between 1990 and 1992, when Lehman Brothers' equity research department was the best on Wall Street, its star analysts attributed their success in large part to the direction and guidance provided by their bosses, Jack Rivkin and Fred Fraenkel. We also found that managers who work for the same boss for a long time stay longer than those who have to constantly adjust to new supervisors.

Internal Networks

By encouraging people to forge relationships across functions and disciplines, companies help them deliver better results. For instance, the research generated by the investment firm Sanford C. Bernstein put the company on the map, but its analysts were able to compete because a strong sales team supported them. The sales representatives communicated the analysts' recommendations to clients and the clients' decisions to the analysts. They also kept the analysts in contact with clients' money managers. Reasoning that clients would never find out about its talented analysts if its salespeople were weak, the firm encouraged analysts to team up with salespeople, and it created a culture that fostered such relationships.

Training

While attending in-house training programs may not add market value to stars, it helps them perform better within the organization. Smart companies use such programs to inform executives about the resources that are available and how best to use them. In fact, the ways executives leverage a company's capabilities often decides who becomes a star—and who does not. For instance, Lehman Brothers' stars greatly valued a 13-week training program the company had created that taught them, among other things, how to structure and format reports. One of the analysts described the program as the "rocket that took them to stardom."

Teams

Despite their egos, stars know that one of the things that distinguishes them from rivals is the quality of their coworkers. For example, star analysts often integrate portfolio strategists' research into their reports, and they feel that its quality is critical to their performance. Many stars also acknowledge that working with smart colleagues sparks ideas that stimulate productivity. Teammates often help stars by counseling and coaching them and serving as role models. A little prodding is sometimes necessary; in order to ingrain a team mentality in the organization, Lehman Brothers stipulated in 1992 that every analyst's presentation had to refer to at least two compatriots. Goldman Sachs's legendary coleader from 1976 to 1985, John Whitehead, once cautioned an analyst: "At Goldman Sachs, we never say 'I.'"

Although many companies have ample resources, good systems, and smart people, executives and professionals often forget that every organization works a little differently. The informal systems through which executives find information and get work done are unique to each company. When stars join new organizations, they must learn about the informal networks and build trust with other people before the systems will work for them. However, stars don't give themselves enough time to get up to speed in new settings because of their egos. They also invest in skills they can use across different companies and don't care about developing their firm-specific knowledge because companies treat them as free agents.

Some corporations are better than others at integrating stars, but it's more important for every company to grow its own stars, even though the process may be time-consuming, expensive, and risky. Not only do home-grown stars tend to outperform imported stars, they are also more loyal. They realize that they outperform rivals in other firms because of their companies' capabilities, so companies only have to develop those competencies in order to retain their stars. As we shall show, companies like Sanford Bernstein and Lehman Brothers were able to grow many stars. They didn't pamper their A players either, since both the star and the organization knew that they were tied to each other. Interestingly, companies like Goldman Sachs, which retained most of the talent it created, were also able to absorb stars when they did hire them.

How Companies Grow Stars

Companies are never explicit about it, but they usually adhere to one of three people-development philosophies. Most firms hire hardworking people, don't do much to develop or retain them, but focus on retaining the high-level stars they bring in from outside. Others recruit smart people and develop some into stars, knowing that they may lose them to rivals. Only a few corporations recruit bright people, develop them into stars, and do everything possible to retain them. American baseball teams are the same: Some franchises hire the best free agents and pay little attention to their farm teams, others have great farm teams but don't hold onto the high-fliers, and a few have good minor league outfits that feed the major league team. Any of those approaches may let a team win the World Series once, but in business, the only viable strategy is to recruit good people, develop them, and retain as many of the stars as possible.

That sounds tough, but it isn't impossible, as companies like Sanford Bernstein and Lehman Brothers demonstrated in the 1990s. They didn't use fancy tricks or shortcuts to develop stars; they were patient about the way they chose people and painstakingly trained them to excel. For instance, Sanford Bernstein took plenty of time to identify the right person for a job. Once the company decided it needed to track an industry, it spent two years, on average, looking for an analyst. If the firm couldn't find a good-enough candidate, it left the position vacant. While Sanford Bernstein used several search firms, none of them were Wall Street headhunters, because the company preferred candidates from business and consulting. As a rule, it avoided hiring from rivals because it believed that even smart youngsters wouldn't be able to change their habits and do things the Bernstein way.

For every analyst position, Sanford Bernstein screened 100 résumés and rigorously interviewed 40 to 50 people. Each candidate visited four to six times and met with

20 to 30 people. Interviewers tried to identify bright, creative, personable people; assessed intellect, quantitative skills, and drive; and tested candidates' ability to adjust to different audiences. CEO Lisa Shalett told us, "The case I've often posed to applicants is: 'The Rolling Stones are going to give a concert in the park. How would we estimate how many people are going to come? Does it matter that it is a free concert?' The answer wasn't as important as the process by which the candidate arrived at one. I try to gauge how tenacious she is. Does she give up easily? Does she come up with a one-word answer?" After the interviews, a human relations expert and a psychologist met with the candidates to evaluate their motivation and ability to fit in with the company culture. Around 20% of the applicants were weeded out because they did not win the experts' approval. Hiring each analyst cost the firm an average of $500,000 to $1 million.

Lehman Brothers' research department, too, used a team-based hiring approach. Several people in the department interviewed each would-be analyst. Fred Fraenkel, the company's global research head from 1990 to 1995, told us: "I tried to figure out whether the candidate had the intellectual capacity and work ethic to become an industry expert. . . . The third issue was whether the interviewee was capable of representing those two qualities to clients, orally or in writing, so that he or she could gain recognition. The fourth was our magic bullet. I asked myself whether the interviewee was someone people were going to like. If he or she wasn't, I would let them go." Jack Rivkin, Lehman

Brothers' research director at the time, was emphatic about whom he would not hire: "I have a no-jerks policy. To me, a jerk is someone difficult to manage, marching to his own drummer, not interested in what is going on in the department and the firm. We are not going to have people like that here." The interviewers usually decided the fate of candidates by consensus; nobody could pull rank, and there was no counting of votes. If any interviewer had concerns that could not be resolved, the firm would pass on the applicant.

Training and mentoring were as important as selection. For instance, participants in Lehman Brothers' 13-week training program ranged from MBA graduates to 50-year-olds who had been analysts with the company for 25 years. The firm's top analysts offered sessions on subjects like analyzing balance sheets, creating something special in your research, and dealing with investment banking. They also offered nuts-and-bolts lessons on how to conduct individual or group meetings, how to deal with different kinds of clients at a group meeting, and how not to say stupid things to the press. In addition to granting recognition to the company's experts, the program made analysts feel they had been initiated into a fraternity, and it strengthened their feeling that Lehman Brothers was a fun place to work.

Not only did Sanford Bernstein and Lehman Brothers turn people into stars, they also managed to retain many of them. The compensation they offered was competitive, but retaining stars requires more than salaries. Aware that stars wanted to broaden their skill bases, the firms encouraged them to do so. For instance, they invited star analysts to speak on behalf of the company at conferences and allowed them to develop relationships with clients. They also publicly recognized star analysts' contributions because the stars needed to feel a sense of achievement. Both companies eased the work/life tension by giving stars flexibility. Lehman Brothers' Rivkin encouraged star analysts to establish home offices so they could spend more time with their families. The analysts so loved working for Rivkin that Lehman Brothers managed to retain them despite paying 25% to 30% less than rivals—a gap that Wall Street dubbed the Rivkin discount. When the firm's work environment changed after Rivkin left in 1992, the company faced an exodus of talent. In a 15-month period that ended in June 1995, 30 of 72 research analysts, including 15 stars, left the company. More recently, Lehman Brothers' current research director, Steve Hash, reintroduced many of the firm's earlier practices, and his department was ranked number one by *Institutional Investor* in 2003.

If You Must Hire Stars . . .

Should companies *ever* hire stars? From 1988 to 1996, only three of 24 investment banks we studied in depth were able to integrate star analysts into their organizations. Our answer is therefore predictable.

Still, let's look at the data. Of the stars hired by the investment banks, 37% were brought on board to enter new businesses, 26% came as replacements for star analysts who had left, 20% were hired to fill the vacated posts of nonstar analysts, and 17% were intended to strengthen existing research teams. The stars whose performance declined the most were those who had been hired to establish new businesses or strengthen teams. The former couldn't cope, we believe, because there were few complementary capabilities they could use, and the latter had to fight the system—that is, the existing team. The performance of the replacements and substitutes did not decline, because they stepped into vacuums and learned to use the companies' resources. Thus, companies can get the most out of outside stars by hiring them either as replacements for departed stars or as a way of raising standards.

It isn't easy to integrate stars into organizations. We found that smart companies identified the attributes of the stars they had created and made sure that the stars they hired had the same qualities. Because much of a star's effectiveness depends on knowledge about and relationships within the organization, the companies targeted stars from similar firms or identified stars whose performance was driven by general skills. The best recruiters didn't shop down the road. They looked far and wide to identify up-and-comers and relatively unknown stars from regional firms, even scouring smaller and global markets.

Only the companies that drew up detailed plans were able to assimilate stars. Take the case of Goldman Sachs, which successfully integrated many of the stars it hired. The company collected a great deal of information, ranging from the performance of recommended stocks to the quality of written research, on every star analyst it hired. It made hiring decisions in consultation with other company functions, such as institutional sales and stock trading. Upon learning that the research department was bringing in a star, the other departments started building a presence in the star's area of expertise before the individual arrived, even if doing so involved recruiting people. Finally, Goldman Sachs's sales force helped the stars package their research reports, and it leveraged its ties to institutional investors to get clients to accept the recommendations quickly.

At the same time, smart companies, aware that it takes time for stars to adjust to new settings, design long-term performance goals. It's important that the deal be structured in such a way as to reward the star's performance and help coworkers cope with his entry. Companies must strike a balance between guaranteed compensation and other incentives. Finally, firms must never forget the stars they already have. Goldman Sachs, for instance, avoided demotivating its homegrown and previously hired stars by offering them and its newcomers the same range of compensation.

Sad to say, many companies don't realize that their human resource philosophies dictate how successful— or unsuccessful—they are at developing stars. Between 1988 and 1996, Sanford Bernstein was able to make a star out of one in five analysts; Merrill Lynch's rate was one in 30. Moreover, it took analysts at Merrill Lynch 12 years, on average, to climb to the top, but at Sanford Bernstein, they did it in four years flat. Was it sheer coincidence that Sanford Bernstein focused on growing stars while Merrill Lynch poached as many as it could from other companies? We don't think so; if companies want to, they can develop stars. Indeed, the first step in winning the war for talent is not to hire stars but to grow them.

Note

1. Klass P. Baks, "On the Performance of Mutual Fund Managers," unpublished manuscript, November 2001.

BORIS GROYSBERG is an assistant professor, **ASHISH NANDA** is an associate professor, and **NITIN NOHRIA** is the Richard P. Chapman Professor of Business Administration at Harvard Business School.

Originally published in May 2004. Reprint R0405F

Growing Talent as if Your Business Depended on It

by Jeffrey M. Cohn, Rakesh Khurana, and Laura Reeves

IN THE THIRTEENTH CENTURY, it took the College of Cardinals almost three years to anoint a successor to Pope Clement IV. To break the stalemate, one of history's most bitter organizational deadlocks, church officials began limiting the food and drink they provided the voting cardinals, eventually giving them just bread and water. Fortunately, today's cardinals don't seem to need such harsh incentives: It took them less than a week to choose Benedict XVI.

When it comes to succession planning (and, by extension, leadership development) in the business world, corporate boards could do with a similar sense of urgency—though we wouldn't necessarily advocate starving them into it. Traditionally, boards have left these tasks very much up to their CEOs and human resources departments. There's a simple reason why directors pay so little attention to these activities: They don't perceive that a lack of leadership development in a company poses the same kind of threat that accounting blunders or missed earnings do.

That's a shortsighted view. Companies whose boards and senior executives fail to prioritize succession planning and leadership development end up either experiencing a steady attrition in talent or retaining people with outdated skills. Such firms become extremely vulnerable when they have to cope with inevitable organizational upheavals—integrating an acquired company with a different operating style and culture, for instance, or reexamining basic operating assumptions when a competitor with a leaner cost structure emerges. In situations like these, businesses need to have the right people in the right roles to survive. But if leadership development has not been a primary focus for CEOs, senior management teams, and boards, their organizations will be more likely to make wrong decisions. Firms may be forced to promote untested, possibly unqualified, junior managers. Or they might have to look outside for executives, who could then find it difficult to adjust to their new companies and cultures.

Some companies, however, have not only recognized the importance of including succession planning and leadership development on the board's agenda but have also taken steps to ensure that those items get on the docket. Over the past three years, we have undertaken extensive fieldwork with many of these companies, conducting multiple interviews and analyzing their

Idea in Brief

Like any manager, you can expect your firm to face periodic upheavals—for example, a major acquisition or the emergence of ominous new competitors. If you don't have the right people in the right roles to guide your company through such choppy waters, you put your company at grave risk. For example, you may be forced to promote untested junior managers or hire outsiders who can't adjust to your company's culture fast enough to successfully lead change.

How to mitigate such risk? Create an **integrated leadership development program**. Unlike stand-alone, ad hoc development activities, an integrated leadership development program is owned by everyone in your organization:

CEOs and VPs develop plans for replacing themselves. Board members actively identify and develop rising stars. Line managers willingly relinquish their best performers to other units so emerging leaders can gain cross-functional experience.

Carefully crafted, your integrated leadership development program becomes a core part of your company's value proposition. You attract talented future leaders, establish the bench strength you need to execute crucial strategic initiatives, and boost shareholder confidence in your firm. And because rivals can't copy your program, it becomes an enduring source of competitive advantage—as giants such as Tyson Foods, Mellon Financial Corporation, and Starbucks have discovered.

varied approaches to successful leadership planning and development. We have found that the best of their programs all share some common attributes. They are not stand-alone, ad hoc activities coordinated by the human resources department; their development initiatives are embedded in the very fabric of the business. From the board of directors on down, senior executives are deeply involved, and line managers are evaluated

Idea in Practice

To create your integrated leadership development program:

Embrace succession planning.

Too many CEOs consider the term "succession planning" taboo—akin to planning their own funeral. To build strong leadership teams, CEOs—and leaders at least three levels below—must embrace succession planning and integrate it closely with management-training and development programs.

> **Example:** When Orin Smith took Starbucks's helm in 2000, he established an exit date of 2005. He recruited Jim Donald as a promising successor. Then he groomed Donald for the CEO position by having him work in stores to understand the customer experience and visit coffee-roasting

plants to observe operations. Eventually shouldering responsibility for North American operations, Donald developed his own succession plan—assessing and developing potential leaders who could take over his assignments and provide the right fit with the leadership team.

Involve the board.

Detached from daily operations and biases, your board of directors can objectively assess your company's leadership development systems and bench strength. Encourage directors to get to know your firm's rising stars: board members will gauge the efficacy of your leadership pipeline, and emerging leaders will gain experience presenting to the top of the house—a key development opportunity.

and promoted expressly for their contributions to the organizationwide effort.

By engaging managers and the board in this way, a company can align its leadership development processes with its strategic priorities. The company can also build a clear and attractive identity; its employees perceive that leadership development processes are what they are declared to be. Such coherence, identity, and

Example: Mellon Financial Corporation once required heads of major business units to give presentations to the board. But starting in 2002, CEO Marty McGuinn began having rising stars make these presentations. Unit managers accompany their emerging leaders to board meetings and answer questions only when absolutely necessary. But the future leaders get the floor.

Insist that managers share top performers.

Motivate unit leaders to share brilliant junior managers with other units. High-potential leaders will gain exposure to your company's operations and see how the organization's parts collaborate to execute strategy. Cross-functional assignments also provide opportunities to master new business challenges, such as managing a turnaround or launching a product in a new territory. These assignments also enable rising stars to broaden their spheres of influence.

Example: At Tyson Foods, unit leaders are held personally accountable for rotating emerging leaders through other parts of the company. The CEO and VP of HR monitor cross-functional development plans and ensure that unit leaders receive equally qualified managers in exchange for their outgoing ones. Tyson also links senior executives' compensation to their ability to circulate and develop emerging leaders.

authenticity, in turn, make it easier for the company to attract the future leaders it needs.

In the following pages, we'll describe what some of the companies we've been observing are doing to create strong, effective succession-planning and leadership development programs. First, let's take a closer look at where many companies go wrong when they set out to grow great managers.

Every Which Way

Tyson Foods, a family-controlled company based in Springdale, Arkansas, provides a good example of where companies can fall short in leadership development. Every time CEO John Tyson, grandson of the company founder with the same name, picked up a journal, newspaper, or business magazine, he saw yet another story of how iconic companies like General Electric set the standard in churning out future leaders, and he was frustrated in his ambition to leave a similar legacy.

It was a big ambition. Despite Tyson's size after its merger with IBP in 2001—the company's market cap was around $25 billion, putting it well into the *Fortune* 100—it had, in its 70 years, invested very little in leadership development. And the organization had no ingrained systems, tools, or processes to ensure a steady supply of qualified talent. When he took the reins in 2000, Tyson had made it his goal to change all that, and the company, over the next two years, experimented with several leadership development initiatives.

These experiments all followed a similar course. Typically, Tyson or a member of his senior management team would read an article or hear about an interesting initiative at another company, such as a mentoring program. Then he or one of his colleagues would chat with Ken Kimbro, the senior vice president of corporate HR, about the possibility of implementing a comparable program at Tyson (the Tyson Mentor Program, for instance). A few weeks later, a Tyson version of the initiative would be discussed in internal focus groups, and pilots would be developed.

One time, John Tyson was invited by the CEO of a prominent company to see how that organization monitored its emerging leaders' progress. When he returned to the offices, he cleared out an entire conference room and plastered on its walls pictures of Tyson's rising-star managers, with descriptions of their job experiences, educational backgrounds, strengths and weaknesses, and development paths. Another time, Tyson personally approved a budget to send the company's high-potential managers to leadership retreats on a remote Rio Grande ranch. The managers worked to solve actual business challenges facing the company, reflected on their personal leadership styles, and broadened their spheres of influence by meeting other high-potentials within the company. For its part, Tyson's HR group found it hard to keep up with the rush of programs.

Despite John Tyson's efforts and the popularity of many of his initiatives, the company's talent pipeline was still not producing enough quality leaders, and by the summer of 2002, the CEO realized that his ad hoc approach to leadership development was not working. He formed a senior executive task force to look into the problem. The team included himself, his direct reports, and a small group of external succession-planning experts, who were there to ensure objectivity and high standards and to help facilitate buy in.

The task force members took nothing for granted. They sat down with a blank sheet of paper and mapped out their ideal leadership development system for

Tyson. The blueprint they came up with integrated succession planning and leadership development, made sure that promising leaders would be well versed in all aspects of the company's business, and put the accountability for succession planning and leadership development squarely on the shoulders of John Tyson's direct reports. "Leaders at all levels were either in or out," Tyson recalled. They couldn't waffle about contributing their time and effort to the new talent development system; they couldn't "protect" talent, hoard resources, or declare themselves immune from succession planning, he said.

An Integrated Approach

Succession planning was the critical starting point for Tyson's new program—as it was for all the leading-edge companies we observed. Succession planning should drive leadership development at a company; that sounds reasonable enough but is hard for many managers to accept. That's because many people, from the CEO on down, consider the word "succession" taboo. Planning your exit is like scheduling your own funeral; it evokes fears and emotions long hidden under layers of defense mechanisms and imperceptible habits. Perversely, the desire to avoid this issue is strongest in the most successful CEOs. Their standard operating procedure is to always look for the next mountain to climb, not to step down from the mountain and look for a replacement.

We recently conducted a leadership and talent management survey with 20 CEOs in large corporations, representing a variety of industries and locations. Although all 20 executives agreed that having the right talent in the right roles was critical for their companies' success and that a talent management program was important for developing effective leaders, almost half had no succession plans for VPs and above. Only one-fourth of the CEOs had talent pipelines that extended at least three managerial levels below them.

Meanwhile, those CEOs who are effective at building strong leadership teams tend not to have any reservations about succession; they embrace succession planning and integrate it closely with the company's management-training and development programs. When Orin Smith became president and CEO of Starbucks in 2000, for instance, he made it a top priority to plan his own succession. He established an exit date—in 2005, at age 62—which helped him push his business agenda. Ultimately, Smith's actions focused attention on emerging leaders throughout the company.

Two years into the job, Smith knew that the internal contenders would still be too unseasoned for the CEO position by his exit date. Starbucks was under pressure to grow its leaders as fast as the business was expanding, from approximately 8,500 global retail locations to about 30,000 sites, half of them outside the United States. Because of his early commitment to succession planning, Smith knew enough about the internal CEO candidates—and decided on an outsider, Jim Donald, as a promising successor. Donald had an established record in supermarket expansion as chairman, president, and CEO of Pathmark, a 143-unit regional grocery chain.

He was recruited to Starbucks specifically to become the next CEO.

Starbucks gave Donald 90 days of dedicated immersion. He worked in the stores to understand the customer experience, and he observed firsthand the operations in the coffee-roasting plants. Then Donald was made responsible for North American operations, Starbucks's largest business. Progressively, he became accountable for more pieces of the company. One of his first major tests was to develop his own succession plan and to execute against it in order to move to a larger role himself. Smith and Starbucks's board members paid close attention to Donald's ability to assess and develop a talented leader who could take over Donald's assignments and provide the right fit with the leadership team.

As Starbucks's experience shows, CEOs need to embrace succession planning to achieve their own legacies and the financial success of the organizations they leave behind. By integrating succession planning and talent development, CEOs can alert the rising stars in their companies to potential leadership opportunities well in advance; and they and their boards can more accurately assess their bench strength. When the process runs smoothly, boards have a strong sense of whether a company's incumbent leadership team will be able to execute important strategic initiatives in the future. The company also gains because of minimal disruption to the business, shareholder confidence and positive analyst ratings, and reduced costs of external hiring for senior executive positions.

The consumer products company S.C. Johnson & Son also uses an integrated approach. Its performance appraisal program identifies the rising stars in the company's hard-to-fill management and technical positions, evaluates them through 360-degree feedback, and determines potential leaders' readiness for promotions. The well-oiled program also includes processes to identify "safe positions"—crucial jobs with reinforced retention strategies and ready replacements. The tight integration of succession planning with talent development has paid off: The typical manager at S.C. Johnson has been on the job for nearly 15 years, and nine out of every ten positions are filled internally.

At Tyson, just a few years after the formation of the initial senior management task force on leadership development, all of John Tyson's direct reports are fully committed to the succession-planning process. In what they call the "talent alignment and optimization" initiative, or TAO, leaders from across the organization try to strike a balance between the supply of talent (rising stars) and the demand for talent (critical positions). Right after Tyson's strategic review process, which is held semiannually, the company's senior management team holds open and constructive discussions about the company's high-potential managers to ensure that the organization nurtures in them the skills necessary to execute current strategy while also preparing them to take on larger, more complex roles. And to make sure that rising stars are challenged and achieve long-term success at Tyson, the senior leaders work closely with

HR to devise development paths that consider multiple career possibilities for high-potentials, three to five years out.

A Line and Board Responsibility

Many executives believe that leadership development is a job for the HR department. This may be the single biggest misconception they can have. As corporations have broken down work into manageable activities and then consolidated capabilities into areas of expertise, employee-related activities have typically fallen into HR's domain. The prevailing wisdom has been that if HR took care of those often intangible "soft" issues, line managers and executives would be free to focus on "hard" business issues and client interaction.

But at companies that are good at growing leaders, operating managers, not HR executives, are at the front line of planning and development. In fact, many senior executives now hold their line managers directly responsible for these activities. In this worldview, it is part of the line manager's job to recognize his subordinates' developmental needs, to help them cultivate new skills, and to provide them opportunities for professional development and personal growth. Managers must do this even if it means nudging their rising stars into new functional areas or business units. They must mentor emerging leaders, from their own and other departments, passing on important knowledge and providing helpful evaluations and feedback. The operating managers' own evaluations, development plans, and promotions, in turn, depend on how successfully they nurture their subordinates.

Line managers are held accountable not only for aiding in the development of individual star managers but also for helping senior executives and HR experts define and create a balanced leadership development system for the entire company. They must tackle questions such as "How will we balance the need to nurture future leaders with the pressures to eliminate redundant activities?" and "How should we encourage burgeoning leaders to take risks and innovate while maintaining our focus on short-term operations and profit goals?" (Firms shouldn't have to forgo their quarterly targets for the sake of developing high-potential managers.) Practical solutions to these and other challenges don't magically appear in HR conference rooms; they come from the line managers.

If line managers are held responsible for executing the talent development initiatives, the board should assume high-level ownership of the overall system. Traditionally, however, most boards have focused on CEO succession, giving short shrift to systematic leadership development. After all, there was little risk of a calamity occurring if the board *didn't* monitor the leadership pipeline. There was also little chance that the board members would be held personally accountable for the resulting weak talent pool. In A.T. Kearney's 2004 survey on the effectiveness of corporate governance, participating board directors universally acknowledged the importance of leadership development and succession planning. Yet only one in four respondents believed the board of directors was very good at these activities.

The CEOs of savvy companies realize that their boards are well placed to help them plan for new leadership to take the reins. Detached from day-to-day operations and biases, board directors can objectively look at the company's leadership development systems and bench strength. At Starbucks, for example, the board oversees a formalized succession-planning process for 2,500 positions. Its goal is to make sure the company always has the right people with the right values in the right places at the right times. As Orin Smith explains: "The values and behaviors of the individuals you choose go through the organization like a rifle shot; they can be felt at the line level within months. We can't afford to hire or promote people with the wrong values. It's a path to mediocrity."

Some boards are becoming aggressive in getting to know their companies' rising stars. Pittsburgh-based Mellon Financial, a 136-year-old financial institution, had long required the heads of its major business units to give presentations to the board. But in 2002, CEO Marty McGuinn saw potential value in having the company's rising stars make these presentations. Now, Mellon's unit managers accompany the rising stars to the board meetings. They answer questions when absolutely necessary, but the future leaders get the floor. As a result, the board can assess for itself the efficacy of the company's leadership pipeline and hear about corporate initiatives from the people who are actually "doing things." Meanwhile, the rising stars gain direct access to the board, gleaning new perspectives and wisdom as a result.

A Shared Resource

No leadership development program can be effective unless it provides mechanisms for exposing future leaders to the full range of the company's operations. By introducing their rising stars to new business units, geographies, and business challenges (managing a turn-around, for instance, or launching a new product in a foreign market), companies can help these executive-track employees broaden their power bases and spheres of influence while giving them a sense of how the different parts of the organization work together to execute the overall corporate strategy.

It's a reasonable goal but hard to accomplish. Why would the supervisor of a brilliant junior manager share that talent with another unit, knowing that productivity and profitability in his own unit might suffer? And what if the rising star misinterprets the transfer to another business unit (with perhaps fewer people and less revenue) as a negative gesture and considers leaving the company?

Tyson Foods faced just such challenges. Under the company's revamped leadership development program, business unit heads were obliged to share their highest-performing managers with other business units so these rising stars could gain cross-functional experience. Initially, it was hard for the unit leaders to do so, after years of hoarding talent and building personal fiefdoms.

To encourage sharing, John Tyson holds the business unit and functional leaders personally accountable for rotating emerging leaders through different parts of the company. Cross-functional development plans—essentially, the road maps for high-potentials' assignments to Tyson's different businesses—are clearly articulated at the succession conferences described earlier. These plans are monitored by Tyson and the vice president of corporate HR. Moreover, the CEO assures unit leaders that they will receive equally qualified managers in exchange for their outgoing ones. The company's talent-assessment practices have been refined so that the right qualities and skills are being measured across all businesses and functions. That is, Tyson realized that a manager's success in one area of the business was by no means a guarantee of success in another. So the company carefully retrofitted its performance assessment tools to measure the competencies, values, and skills that would be necessary for any future positions that a manager might pursue. The results are objective, so business unit leaders are exchanging "apples for apples," not simply sending B players to other units and keeping their fingers crossed for a star in return. Tyson has also adopted formal performance-management review policies that link senior executive compensation to the movement and development of emerging leaders.

Mellon's Marty McGuinn has a similar philosophy. His strikingly simple but powerful mantra is "Connect the dots." That is, for Mellon to create a leadership development system that competitors cannot match,

A Leadership Development Checklist

TO GROW GREAT LEADERS, companies should do the following:

- Launch a formal, high-level succession-planning conference for senior executives facilitated by corporate HR and outside experts; outline the leadership development process; and cascade it through the company.

- Create leadership development programs that fill holes in your company's talent portfolio to ensure a deep bench for critical positions in the firm.

- Let HR create tools and facilitate their use, but require the business units to own the leadership development activities.

- Have the board oversee all leadership development initiatives, and insist on continual communication by CEOs and other senior managers on their commitment to leadership development.

- Reshuffle rising stars throughout the company, taking care that A players are exchanged for other A players.

- Make sure that your leadership development program is aligned with your strategy, reinforces your company's brand, and has support from your employees.

all its managers must map their discrete leadership development activities and processes to a coherent, companywide system. Managers in dramatically different functions, locations, and operating units are expected to share knowledge and talent that they think would enhance the whole system. (The sidebar "A Crash Course" describes how Mellon built its integrated leadership development system.)

A Crash Course

MOST OF THE COMPANIES we studied developed their leadership programs over time or at least were under relatively little pressure in terms of talent management. Mellon Financial, however, had to build a new system under extreme pressure to support senior management's efforts to transform the company.

By the late 1990s, the venerable organization comprised a wide range of businesses. The senior management team had articulated a business strategy that focused on high-growth opportunities and global expansion. Through the disposition of specific units, and through strategic acquisitions to build its asset management and corporate and institutional services businesses, senior management effectively transformed Mellon from a traditional commercial bank to a more focused financial services institution.

But CEO Marty McGuinn realized that the next generation of leaders would not be able to execute the new strategy without an enhanced set of competencies and a broader, more entrepreneurial mind-set, one that could include bundling products and services, cross selling to clients, and expanding into unproven global markets.

To meet this challenge, Mellon's HR department created an extensive leadership development program that was rolled out to the whole company. Mellon's senior management team was involved from the start. McGuinn and his team met frequently (in person and via e-mail) and conducted one-on-one discussions with emerging

Aligned, Attractive, and Authentic

As Tyson learned, an effective talent development program is more than just a portfolio of off-the-shelf components such as competency-profiling tools, 360-degree feedback, and online training. It is a carefully thought-out system that you have to develop for yourself.

leaders at the company. Armed with these data, the executives helped Mellon's rising stars understand the competencies they would need and developed plans for them to acquire those skills.

But McGuinn and Mellon's human resources director knew that HR's tools for leadership development would not gain traction among managers if they were not owned and implemented by the business units. Mellon's managers had a reputation for being results driven and focused on achieving day-to-day goals. An HR-mandated mentoring program or 360-degree feedback assessment initiative, no matter how shiny and slick, might seem like a distraction to these people—and would ultimately be futile.

McGuinn, therefore, instituted a policy that leadership development tools would be created in formal centers of excellence consisting of three to six resident experts. The tools would then be offered to the business units through a specialized distribution network of human resources business partners (HRBP)—liaisons between the centers of excellence and the business unit heads. The HRBPs were charged with understanding the strategies of the business units and the competencies they wanted to develop and execute. The HRBPs would use that information to determine, in collaboration with the unit leaders, which leadership development tools to use. Because the units' strategies varied considerably across Mellon, McGuinn and HR granted the HRBPs wide latitude in their decisions about how, when, and why to use particular tools.

As a CEO assessing a new program, the first question you need to ask yourself is whether the constituent parts of your program combine to enable the company to compete more effectively. A company that operates in a highly innovative environment, for example, needs to know whether its leadership development system actually enables it to produce better innovations more quickly than its competitors. If the system rewards individuals who produce the most predictable rather than the most innovative results, it is misaligned.

Misalignment usually occurs when companies have developed, tested, and rolled out initiatives ad hoc, without any high-level planning or a defined time horizon. The first iteration of Tyson's mentoring program, for instance, was barely linked to the company's existing leadership development activities and strategic goals. Little thought went into the matching process; rising stars weren't necessarily assigned mentors in the businesses and functions that could have helped them the most, so significant developmental opportunities were lost.

Misalignment can also occur when a company's 360-degree feedback and performance-management instruments measure (and reward) behaviors that are inconsistent with the company's values and culture. It may be counterproductive, for instance, to reward managers for their skills in acquiring new customers if the company's overall strategy is to focus on existing customers by cross selling and offering bundled products and services.

The second question you need to ask is whether your leadership development system reinforces the perceptions you want people to have about the company. We've found that there is a direct relationship between a strongly defined leadership development program at a company and the types of job candidates the company attracts, external stakeholders' perceptions of the business, and employees' understanding of the firm's values and strategies. For example, Starbucks employees, all of whom are called "partners," are attracted to the job in part because of the company's talent identity. They want to be that cheerful, smiling-to-the-music person behind the counter who helps customers start the day out right with a *venti* or a *grande*. The company's leadership development program reinforces this identity: Its hiring and promotion processes put equal weight on an employee's functional capabilities and his or her ability to fit in with the company's values and beliefs system. And to preserve the company's culture in this time of rapid growth, Starbucks has added a component to the program, called Leading from the Heart, which helps existing managers transmit Starbucks's customer-friendly (and brand-centric) ethos to new hires.

The third question you have to ask is whether your employees think the company's leadership programs are legitimate. They will take the program seriously only if they know these talent management elements will affect actual business decisions instead of just padding personnel folders. They must also believe that those individuals whom the system recruits, selects, and promotes are truly qualified for their positions and aren't just being rewarded for their political allegiances.

Companies need to address the issue of authenticity head-on. Senior executives at Mellon realized that some people might be skeptical about the company's new talent development initiatives: Many managers felt they were too busy dealing with day-to-day operations and client relations to take time off to attend the company's mentoring program. Recognizing this skepticism, HR included in the sessions case studies of mentoring relationships and how they helped to improve results on the job. (The sessions themselves are data driven and led by senior operating executives.) Specifically, the sessions demonstrate the positive correlation between the productive relationships a manager can have with his or her team members and the economic effectiveness of that group or division. Most executives find it a compelling proposition that, with help from the mentoring program, they can actively improve their employees' skills, increase people's commitment to work, boost information sharing, and create better-trained employees who are willing to accept greater responsibility.

The companies that shared their stories and knowledge with us highlighted several critical aspects of leadership development—in particular, CEOs' awareness and acknowledgment of the importance of succession planning; boards' increased activity in system oversight; managers' refocused attention on people issues and processes; and HR's role in facilitating the entire organization's ownership of leadership development. As their experiences demonstrate, a leadership development program need not be a ragbag of training programs and benefits. Properly thought through, it can be a major part of a company's value proposition—one that competitors can't even understand, much less copy.

Note

Our colleague Gianni Montezemolo passed away just before this article was published. We'd like to thank him for his contributions to this research.

JEFFREY M. COHN is the president of Bench Strength Advisors in New York and a former Harvard Business School research associate. **RAKESH KHURANA** is an associate professor of organizational behavior at Harvard Business School. **LAURA REEVES** is a senior manager with the global management consultancy A.T. Kearney's transformation practice in Atlanta.

Originally published in October 2005. Reprint R0510C

How to Keep Your Top Talent

by Jean Martin and Conrad Schmidt

PRACTICALLY EVERY COMPANY THESE days has some form of program designed to nurture its rising stars. With good reason—these high-achieving individuals can have an enormous impact on business results.

Programs aimed at this class of talent are usually organized around some sort of annual nomination process and offer targeted leadership-development opportunities such as business rotations and special stretch assignments. But despite the prevalence of these programs, most haven't delivered much in the way of results. Our recent research on leadership transitions demonstrates that nearly 40% of internal job moves made by people identified by their companies as "high potentials" end in failure.

Moreover, disengagement within this cohort of employees has been remarkably high since the start of the recession: In a September 2009 survey by the Corporate Executive Board, one in three emerging stars reported feeling disengaged from his or her company.

Even more striking, 12% of all the high potentials in the companies we studied said they were actively searching for a new job—suggesting that as the economy rebounds and the labor market warms up, organizations may see their most promising employees take flight in large numbers.

Why do companies so often end up with a shortfall in their talent pipeline? And what distinguishes organizations that have been able to prepare their rising stars for postpromotion success? Working directly with human resources officers, we and our research team at the Corporate Leadership Council have examined current practices to identify what works (and what does not). We have studied more than 20,000 employees dubbed "emerging stars" in more than 100 organizations worldwide over the past six years, exploring how they viewed their employers, how they were managed, and how they reacted to changes in the economy.

Throughout different industries and countries, and in both booms and busts, our findings were consistent: With startling clarity, they showed that most management teams stumble badly when they try to develop their next generation of leaders. Senior managers tend to make misguided assumptions about these employees and take actions on their behalf that actually hinder their development. In isolation or in combination, these mistakes can doom a company's talent investments to irrelevance—or worse. In this article we'll take a closer look at the six most common errors, and by highlighting what some organizations are doing right, we'll show what can be done to correct them.

Idea in Brief

Practically every company these days has some form of program designed to nurture high-potential employees. But a recent study by the Corporate Executive Board demonstrates that nearly 40% of internal job moves made by people identified by their companies as "high potentials" end in failure. Disengagement within this cohort of employees also is remarkable: One in three emerging stars reported feeling disengaged from his or her company. Even more striking, 12% of all the high potentials in the study said they were actively searching for a new job—suggesting that as the economy rebounds and the labor market warms up, organizations may see their most promising employees take flight in large numbers. Why do companies have so much trouble bringing along their next generation of leaders? The Corporate Executive Board's research showed that senior managers make misguided assumptions about these employees and take actions on their behalf that actually hinder their development. When dealing with high-potential employees, firms tend to make six common errors: assuming that all of them are highly engaged, equating current performance with future potential, delegating the management of high potentials down in the organization, shielding promising employees from early derailment, expecting stars to share the pain of organization-wide cutbacks, and failing to link high potentials and their careers to corporate strategy. These mistakes can doom a company's talent investments to irrelevance—or worse.

Mistake 1: Assuming That High Potentials Are Highly Engaged

You've assembled the newest crop of candidates for your fast track, and your CEO is about to step forward to address the group. The room is filled with bright, shining talent. It would seem fair to assume that this group, of all the crowds you could have assembled, comprises people who are enthusiastic about your company. But if your young stars are anything like those at the companies we've studied:

- One in four intends to leave your employ within the year.

- One in three admits to not putting all his effort into his job.

- One in five believes her personal aspirations are quite different from what the organization has planned for her.

- Four out of 10 have little confidence in their coworkers and even less confidence in the senior team.

Why all the negativity? Our study of this group suggests two main reasons: outsized expectations and lots of alternatives. Many of these employees set an incredibly high bar for their organizations. Precisely because they work harder (and often better) than their peers, they expect their organizations to treat them well—by providing them with stimulating work, lots of recognition, compelling career paths, and the chance to prosper if the organization does. So when the organization is struggling—as most are these days—your star players are the first to be disappointed. Meanwhile, they are much more confident than their rank-and-file peers about their ability to find new jobs and are much less passive about researching other opportunities. As a result, when organizations cut back and ask employees to "tough it out," the stars will be the first to say, "No thanks. I'd rather find an employer who appreciates the high level of contributions I'm making."

The downturn has also taken a measurable toll on morale. Since 2007, when companies began adjusting their strategies and curbing spending in response to the weakening economy, employee engagement has plunged. The number of employees who can be described as "highly disengaged"—those most critical of their coworkers, admittedly reducing their effort, and looking for new employment opportunities—has more than doubled, from 8% in the first half of 2007 to 21% at the end of 2009. And as noted earlier, that figure is especially high among star players.

The disenchantment of high potentials has troubling implications for companies. In our research, we found that discretionary effort (that crucial willingness to go above and beyond) can be as much as 50% lower among highly disengaged employees than among their colleagues with average engagement. No CEO, especially in the current environment, can afford to lose so much productivity from a company's core contributors.

It may seem obvious, but the solution is for senior management to double (or even triple) its efforts to keep young stars engaged. That means recognizing them early and often, explicitly linking their individual goals to corporate ones, and letting them help solve the company's biggest problems.

It also means regularly taking the temperature of these valuable employees. In China's rapidly growing market, where finding and retaining talent is especially challenging, multinationals are paying careful attention to their satisfaction. Shell has appointed career stewards who meet regularly with emerging leaders, assess their level of engagement, help them set realistic career expectations, and make sure they're getting the right development opportunities. Executives at Novartis have created a simple checklist to get a read on how crucial employees in China are feeling. Managers rate their relationships with those employees and stars' happiness with their jobs, career opportunities, and work-life balance. The checklist raises the red flags—and managers, with support from the company's HR team, address them quickly.

Even when the bonus pool is running dry, companies can still get up-and-coming talent excited. One retail company rewards its stars by running banner ads celebrating their successes on its intranet, offering them telecommuting or other flexible work options, and even naming companywide initiatives after them. A large manufacturer we studied gives its rising stars privileged access to online discussion boards, led by the CEO, that are dedicated to the company's biggest challenges. Emerging leaders are encouraged to visit the boards daily to share ideas and opinions and to raise their hands for assignments. The site not only boosts their involvement and captures innovative ideas but also gives the CEO and other senior leaders a direct line to the company's best and brightest.

Mistake 2: Equating Current High Performance with Future Potential

The "high potential" designation is often used, at least in part, as a reward for an employee's contribution in a current role. But most people on your leadership track will be asked to deliver future results in much bigger jobs—a consideration that often gets overlooked when senior management anoints elite talent.

It's true that not many low performers have high potential. But it's wrong to assume that most high performers do. Our research shows that more than 70% of today's top performers lack critical attributes essential to their success in future roles. The practical effect of this is that the bulk of talent investments are being wasted on individuals whose potential is not all that high.

What are the attributes that best define rising stars? Our analysis pinpoints three that really matter: ability, engagement, and aspiration. *Ability* is the most obvious attribute. To be successful in progressively more important roles, employees must have the intellectual, technical, and emotional skills (both innate and learned) to handle increasingly complex challenges. No less important, however, is *engagement*—the level of personal connection and commitment the employee feels toward the firm and its mission. As suggested earlier, this attribute should not be taken for granted—and just asking employees if they are satisfied with their jobs isn't enough. Instead, try this simple but powerful question: "What would cause you to take a job with another company tomorrow?" This query prompts people to share their underlying criteria for job satisfaction and to list which of those elements are missing.

Similarly, managers should not make assumptions about promising employees' levels of *aspiration*. This third critical attribute—the desire for recognition, advancement, and future rewards, and the degree to which what the employee wants aligns with what the company wants for him or her—can be extremely difficult to measure. In our experience, it is best to be direct with high-potential candidates, asking pointed questions about what they aspire to and at what price: How far do you hope to rise in the company? How quickly? How much recognition would be optimal? How much money? And so on. (Of course, these responses should be balanced against individuals' "softer" objectives involving work-life balance, job stress, and geographic mobility.)

Shortcomings in even one of the three attributes can dramatically reduce candidates' chances for ultimate success. (See the sidebar "The Ways High Performers Can Fall Short.") And the cost of misidentifying talent can be high. You might, for instance, invest dollars and time in a star who jumps ship just as you are looking for her to take the lead on a project or problem.

Senior leaders need to find a good way to assess top performers on each of the three dimensions. (See "Measuring Employee Potential.") Companies such as AMN Healthcare have done just that—building their annual talent-assessment processes around measures for ability, engagement, and aspiration. Last year, as part of its annual succession-planning process, AMN

10 Critical Components of a Talent-Development Program

IN OUR RESEARCH, WE uncovered a core set of best practices for identifying and managing emerging talent.

Explicitly test candidates in three dimensions: ability, engagement, and aspiration.

Emphasize future competencies needed (derived from corporate-level growth plans) more heavily than current performance when you're choosing employees for development.

Manage the quantity and quality of high potentials at the corporate level, as a portfolio of scarce growth assets.

Forget rote functional or business-unit rotations; place young leaders in intense assignments with precisely described development challenges.

Identify the riskiest, most challenging positions across the company, and assign them directly to rising stars.

Create individual development plans; link personal objectives to the company's plans for growth, rather than to generic competency models.

Reevaluate top talent annually for possible changes in ability, engagement, and aspiration levels.

Offer significantly differentiated compensation and recognition to star employees.

Hold regular, open dialogues between high potentials and program managers, to monitor star employees' development and satisfaction.

Replace broadcast communications about the company's strategy with individualized messagses for emerging leaders—with an emphasis on how their development fits into the company's plans.

The Ways High Performers Can Fall Short

THE SOBERING TRUTH IS that only about 30% of today's high performers are, in fact, high potentials. The remaining 70% may have what it takes to win now but lack some critical component for future success. Indeed, our analysis suggests that individuals in this latter group fit into one of three common archetypes:

1. **Engaged Dreamers.** Engaged dreamers have high levels of engagement and aspiration, but insufficient ability to succeed in more challenging roles. Only about 7% of current high performers fall into this category. Unless the organization can significantly—and quickly—raise these employees' talent and skill levels, the probability that they will succeed at the next level is effectively zero.

2. **Disengaged Stars.** Frighteningly, more than 30% of today's high performers suffer from a lack of engagement. They have the ability and aspiration to be high potentials but are insufficiently committed to the organization to be prudent bets for long-term success. Indeed, employees who exhibit this

Healthcare conducted interviews with more than 200 rising leaders, specifically to get a read on their engagement and aspiration levels. This information, combined with managers' assessments of ability, gives AMN a clear picture of its bench strength. "Our executive committee has far more confidence in the employees identified as high potentials since we started using this model," says Laurie Jerome, the company's vice president of learning and talent development.

profile have only a 13% chance of succeeding at the next level. This group represents a sizable opportunity, however: Organizations can heavily influence employees' engagement levels—if they're paying attention.

3. **Misaligned Stars.** This group accounts for 33% of current high performers. Misaligned stars have both the ability and engagement needed to successfully take on more critical responsibilities, but either don't aspire to the roles available at more senior levels or don't choose to make the sacrifices required to attain and perform those high-level jobs. Their lack of aspiration is less damaging to their potential than a lack of engagement or ability, as evidenced by their 44% chance of success at the next level. But organizations must triage them to separate those whose aspirations might change from those whose long-term career and personal goals would be better accommodated in another organization.

Mistake 3: Delegating Down the Management of Top Talent

It's easy to understand why most companies do this: Line managers know their people best and have a very concrete view of their strengths and weaknesses. Most organizations also recognize the economic benefit of delegating talent management to line leaders—when corporate and HR budgets are limited, it shifts the costs of development programs from headquarters into the budgets of business units.

Measuring Employee Potential

DRAWING ON ITS WORK with corporations over the past decade, the Corporate Leadership Council has developed several ways to measure the three core qualities of potential—ability, engagement, and aspiration. We've combined them in a process we call HIPO-ID. At the heart of this process is a set of questions for candidates and their managers. An abbreviated version of this tool is at www.executive-board.com /humancapital/CLC-highpotential. html. Readers can use it to assess their own employees' potential.

That said, it is a bad idea to delegate management of high potentials to line managers. These employees are a long-term corporate asset and must be managed accordingly. When you leave the task of identifying and cultivating tomorrow's leaders exclusively to the business units, here's what tends to happen: Candidates are selected solely on the basis of recent performance. They are offered narrow development opportunities that are limited by the business units' scope of requirements and focus mostly on skills required now rather than tomorrow. Talented employees can also be hoarded by line managers—collected and protected and certainly not shared.

Responsibility for high potentials' development must be shared by general managers. Johnson & Johnson's LeAD program offers a great example of this approach. As part of J&J's organizational and talent review process, the company's managers select individuals they believe could run a business (or a bigger business) in the next three years to participate in LeAD. The program lasts nine months in total. During this time, participants receive advice and regular assessments from a series of coaches brought in from outside the company. They also must develop a growth project—a new product, service, or business model—intended to create value for their individual units. Each candidate's progress in this regard is evaluated during a leadership session that is held in an emerging market such as China, India, or Brazil in order to increase participants' global knowledge. Graduates leave the program with a multiyear individual development plan and are periodically reviewed by a group of senior HR heads for further development and reassignment across the corporation.

J&J managers believe that the LeAD process has accelerated individual development. "More than half of the LeAD participants have already moved on to bigger positions in the company, and the program has been in existence just three years," says Corey Seitz, vice president of global talent management at the company. One program participant told us, "It was an incredible experience—one that will certainly improve my ability to lead and contribute to J&J." The company has found that when top talent is seen as a critical organizational asset to be developed by senior leaders across the firm—and made to feel like right-hand partners to management—the group's ability and willingness to contribute to the firm dramatically increases.

Mistake 4: Shielding Rising Stars from Early Derailment

In many talent-development programs, a central concern is derailment—or the failure or underperformance of a candidate at the next level. Human resources executives and line managers alike will go to great lengths to ensure that employees with promise are placed in training assignments that provide a bit of a stretch but little real risk of failure. That's understandable; they want to avoid disrupting the business. So most high-potential rotation programs rely on an annual session in which open positions at that point of the calendar year are matched to candidates with the best chances of success. These rotations typically cover various functions and business units—under controllable levels of danger to all concerned.

By being too cautious, however, HR executives and managers can thwart employees' development and put the business at greater risk in the long term: Emerging talent is never truly developed and tested, and the firm finds itself with a sizable cadre of middle and senior managers who can't shoulder the demands of the company's most challenging (and promising) opportunities.

True leadership development takes place under conditions of real stress—"the experience within the experience," as one executive told us. Indeed, the very best programs place emerging leaders in "live fire" roles where new capabilities can—or, more accurately, must—be acquired.

A great example here is Procter & Gamble. Several years ago managers in the company's flagship Family Care division identified a set of complex, high-impact positions that offered particularly quick development and learning—for instance, "brand manager for a leading product" or "director of marketing for a new segment or region." Division managers dubbed these "crucible roles" and began a concerted effort to fill 90% of them with high potentials. Candidates had to pass through three screens to be eligible: They had to have adequate qualifications to perform well in the particular crucible role, stellar leadership skills, and a clear developmental gap the crucible role could help fill.

Through this program, P&G has measurably increased the percentage of employees qualified for promotion: More than 80% of P&G's high-potential employees are ready to take on critical leadership roles each year—putting the company at a tremendous talent advantage when the going gets tough.

Mistake 5: Expecting Star Employees to Share the Pain

Great leaders elect to suffer alongside the rank and file—and sometimes more, in the tradition of the captain who goes down with the ship. So it might seem that your star employees would embrace that same sense of honor and duty. Not so fast. Particularly in difficult business environments, the decision by a senior executive team to freeze or cut salaries and performance-based compensation across the board may seem fair, but it erodes the engagement of the stars. (Recall that one of the most important factors determining a rising star's engagement is the sense that he or she is being recognized—primarily through pay.) The head of human resources at a leading U.S. financial services firm recently bemoaned to us the general unwillingness of his firm's business leaders to differentiate among employees' performances and to direct scarce merit pay to the highest-performing and highest-potential people. Such well-intentioned egalitarianism is a critical mistake.

Our research indicates that under normal circumstances, high potentials put in 20% more effort than other employees in the same roles. Their contributions may be even larger in constrained organizations, where stars tend to be carrying a disproportionate share of the workload because of recent downsizing efforts or restructuring. When you consider that—alongside our discovery (through conversations with recruiting executives) that many firms are actively creating "hit lists" of talent they can target at other firms, and the data showing a significant drop in "intent to stay" scores among top employees—an alarming picture emerges.

During tight fiscal times, it actually costs less to create meaningful differentiation in compensation—even without the jet fuel of (now out-of-favor) stock options. Modest cash or restricted stock grants go further than before, and rank-and-file expectations with respect to merit pay have never been lower. One manufacturing firm recently dedicated a proportion of the dollars saved through layoffs to sweetening the bonus pool for emerging leaders, in order to stave off attrition among them. A retail company we studied has altered salespeople's compensation plans so that high potentials can reap more of what they sow: It doubles the commission salespeople receive for every dollar sold above their annual goal. And another, smaller manufacturing firm we observed has been quietly buying its high potentials lunch every day this year. Even modest signals can go a long way toward helping talent feel appreciated.

Some executives worry that by giving A players special treatment, they may be creating the perception of a "favored class" at the organization. Indeed, 60% of the firms we studied say they avoid using the "high potential" label publicly. But that doesn't mean companies shouldn't make emerging stars feel special. Our research suggests that even employees who haven't been dubbed high potentials work harder (and seem happier) in a system in which good things (raises, promotions, and the like) happen to the people who deserve them. The bottom line: An employee's rewards should be in line with his or her contributions. And if you're treating everyone equally, you're not doing enough to support and keep the people who matter most.

Mistake 6: Failing to Link Your Stars to Your Corporate Strategy

High potentials are acutely aware of the health of the firm and are rightly focused on the acuity of the senior team's strategy. In fact, our research shows that their confidence in their managers—and in their firms' strategic capabilities—is one of the strongest factors in top employees' engagement. An organization that goes "radio silent" with respect to its strategy—or, even worse, explicitly or implicitly signals a strategy freeze in the midst of economic uncertainty—runs the risk of disengaging its rising stars just when they are needed most.

Firms have developed a number of ways to share their future strategies on a privileged basis with their young leaders and to emphasize their role in making that future real. Some companies send them e-mail updates detailing firm performance and strategic shifts; some invite them to quarterly meetings with high-level executives; and some provide access to an online portal where the company's strategy is outlined and critical metrics can be viewed. A global information services firm we've studied gives its high potentials access to a website that allows them to serve as a kind of "shadow board"—weighing in (and even voting) on corporate direction. As part of its Key Talent Programs, HP offers high potentials the opportunity to attend closed-door briefings on important strategic issues, work in teams to help resolve them, and discuss their final recommendations with senior leaders at the company.

A firm's most talented staffers can have meaningful effects across the business. But when burgeoning talent is misidentified, unchallenged, or unrewarded, these individuals become a drag on overall performance. Even worse, their disengagement and eventual derailment can lead to depleted leadership ranks and damage employee commitment and retention across the firm.

Senior executives need to reinforce the message that the "high potential" designation is not primarily an acknowledgment of past accomplishment but mainly an assessment of future contribution. Their talent-management initiatives must challenge and cultivate rising stars, not just celebrate today's high achievements. As the head of HR at one technology firm told us, "These are the people who will launch new businesses, find new ways to strip out costs, build better customer relationships, and drive innovation. Really, the future of our organization is in their hands."

JEAN MARTIN is the executive director and **CONRAD SCHMIDT** is the chief research officer of the Corporate Executive Board's Corporate Leadership Council in Washington, DC.

Originally published in May 2010. Reprint R1005B

Job Sculpting

The Art of Retaining Your Best People

by Timothy Butler and James Waldroop

HIRING GOOD PEOPLE IS TOUGH, but as every senior executive knows, keeping them can be even tougher. Indeed, most executives can tell a story or two about a talented professional who joined their company to great fanfare, added enormous value for a couple of years, and then departed unexpectedly. Usually such exits are written off. "She got an offer she couldn't refuse," you hear, or, "No one stays with one company for very long these days."

Our research over the past 12 years strongly suggests that quite another dynamic is frequently at work. Many talented professionals leave their organizations because senior managers don't understand the psychology of work satisfaction; they assume that people who excel at their work are necessarily happy in their jobs. Sounds logical enough. But the fact is, strong skills don't always reflect or lead to job satisfaction. Many professionals, particularly the leagues of 20-and 30-somethings streaming out of today's MBA programs, are so well educated and achievement oriented that they could succeed in virtually any job. But will they stay?

The answer is, only if the job matches their *deeply embedded life interests.* These interests are not hobbies—opera, skiing, and so forth—nor are they topical enthusiasms, such as Chinese history, the stock market, or oceanography. Instead, deeply embedded life interests are long-held, emotionally driven passions, intricately entwined with personality and thus born of an indeterminate mix of nature and nurture. Deeply embedded life interests do not determine what people are good at—they drive what kinds of activities make them happy. At work, that happiness often translates into commitment. It keeps people engaged, and it keeps them from quitting.

In our research, we found only eight deeply embedded life interests for people drawn to business careers. (For a description of each one, see the sidebar "The Big Eight" at the end of this article.) Life interests start showing themselves in childhood and remain relatively stable throughout our lives, even though they may manifest themselves in different ways at different times. For instance, a child with a nascent deeply embedded life interest in *creative production*—a love for inventing or starting things, or both—may be drawn to writing stories and plays. As a teenager, the life interest might express itself in a hobby of devising mechanical gadgets or an extracurricular pursuit of starting a high school sports or literary magazine. As an adult, the creative-production life interest might bubble up as a drive to be an entrepreneur or a design engineer. It might even show itself as a love for stories again—pushing the person toward a career in, say, producing movies.

Idea in Brief

Hiring good people is tough, but keeping them can be even tougher. The professionals streaming out of today's MBA programs are so well educated and achievement oriented that they could do well in virtually any job. But will they stay? According to noted career experts Timothy Butler and James Waldroop, only if their jobs fit their deeply embedded life interests—that is, their long-held, emotionally driven passions. Butler and Waldroop identify the eight different life interests of people drawn to business careers and introduce the concept of job sculpting, the art of matching people to jobs that resonate with the activities that make them truly happy. Managers don't need special training to job sculpt, but they do need to listen more carefully when employees describe what they like and dislike about their jobs. Once managers and employees have discussed deeply embedded life interests—ideally, during employee performance reviews—they can work together to customize future work assignments. In some cases, that may mean simply adding another assignment to existing responsibilities. In other cases, it may require moving that employee to a new position altogether. Skills can be stretched in many directions, but if they are not going in the right direction—one that is congruent with deeply embedded life interests—employees are at risk of becoming dissatisfied and uncommitted. And in an economy where a company's most important asset is the knowledge, energy, and loyalty of its people, that's a large risk to take.

Think of a deeply embedded life interest as a geo thermal pool of superheated water. It will rise to the surface in one place as a hot spring and in another as a geyser. But beneath the surface—at the core of the individual—the pool is constantly bubbling. Deeply embedded life interests always seem to find expression, even if a person has to change jobs—or careers—for that to happen.

Job sculpting is the art of matching people to jobs that allow their deeply embedded life interests to be expressed. It is the art of forging a customized career path in order to increase the chance of retaining talented people. Make no mistake—job sculpting is challenging; it requires managers to play both detective and psychologist. The reason: many people have only a dim awareness of their own deeply embedded life interests. They may have spent their lives fulfilling other people's expectations of them, or they may have followed the most common career advice: "Do what you're good at." For example, we know of a woman who, on the basis of her skill at chemistry in college, was urged to become a doctor. She complied and achieved great success as a neurologist, but at age 42 she finally quit to open a nursery school. She loved children, demonstrating a deeply embedded life interest in *counseling and mentoring.* And more important, as it turned out, she was also driven by a life interest in *enterprise control,* the desire to be in charge of an organization's overall operations. It was a long time before she stopped remarking, "All those years wasted."

Other people don't know their own deeply embedded life interests because they have taken the path of least resistance: "Well, my dad was a lawyer." Or they've simply been unaware of many career choices at critical points in their lives. Most college seniors and new MBAs set sail on their careers knowing very little about all the possible islands in the sea. And finally, some people end up in the wrong jobs because they have chosen, for reasons good and bad, to follow the siren songs of financial reward or prestige. Regardless of the reason, the fact is that a good number of people,

It's a Matter of Degree

OVER THE PAST SEVERAL DECADES, countless studies have been conducted to discover what makes people happy at work. The research almost always focuses on three variables: ability, values, and life interests. In this article, we argue that life interests are paramount—but what of the other two? Don't they matter? The answer is yes, but less so.

Ability—meaning the skills, experience, and knowledge a person brings to the job—can make an employee feel competent. That's important; after all, research has shown that a feeling of incompetence hinders creativity, not to mention productivity. But although competence can certainly help a person get hired, its effect is generally short lived. People who are good at their jobs aren't necessarily engaged by them.

In the context of career satisfaction, values refer to the rewards people seek. Some people value money, others want intellectual challenge, and still others desire prestige or a comfortable lifestyle. People with the same abilities and life interests may pursue different careers based on their values. Take three people who excel at and love quantitative analysis. One might pursue a career as a professor of finance for the intellectual challenge. Another might go straight to Wall Street to reap the financial rewards. And a third might pursue whatever job track leads to the CEO's office—driven by a desire for power and influence.

Like ability, values matter. In fact, people rarely take jobs that don't match their values. A person who hates to travel would not jump at an offer from a management consulting firm. Someone who values financial security won't chase a career as an independent contractor. But people can be drawn into going down career paths because they have the ability and like the rewards—even though they're not interested in the work. After a short period of success, they become disenchanted, lose interest, and either quit or just work less productively.

That's why we have concluded that life interests are the most important of the three variables of career satisfaction. You can be good at a

(continued)

153

job—indeed, you generally need to be—and you can like the rewards you receive from it. But only life interests will keep most people happy and fulfilled over the long term. And that's the key to retention.

---

at least up until midlife, don't actually know what kind of work will make them happy. (For more on the importance of life interests, abilities, and values in job satisfaction, see the sidebar "It's a Matter of Degree.")

Let's return to Mark, the lending officer at a West Coast bank. Mark was raised in San Francisco; his mother and father were doctors who fully expected their son to become a successful professional. In high school, Mark received straight A's. He went on to attend Princeton, where he majored in economics. Soon after graduation, he began working at a prestigious management consulting firm, where he showed great skill at his assignments: building financial spreadsheets and interpreting pro formas. As expected, Mark left the consulting firm to attend a respected business school and then afterward joined the bank. It was located near his family, and because of its size and growth rate, he thought it would offer him good opportunities for advancement.

Mark, not surprisingly, excelled at every task the bank gave him. He was smart and knew no other way to approach work than to give it his all. But over time, Mark grew more and more unhappy. He was a person who loved running his mind over and through theoretical and strategic what-ifs. (After college, Mark had seriously considered a career in academia but had been dissuaded by his parents.) Indeed, one of Mark's deeply embedded life interests was *theory development and conceptual thinking.* He could certainly excel at the nitty-gritty number crunching and the customer service that his lending job entailed, but those activities did nothing for his heart and soul, not to mention for his commitment to the organization.

Fortunately for both Mark and the bank, he was able to identify what kind of work truly excited him before he quit. Consulting a career counselor, Mark came to see what kind of work interested him and how that differed from his current job responsibilities. Using this insight, he was able to identify a role in the bank's new market development area that would bring his daily tasks in line with his deeply embedded interests. Mark's work now consists of competitive analysis and strategy formulation. He is thriving, and the bank is reaping the benefit of his redoubled energy—and his loyalty.

Career Development: Standard Operating Procedure

As we've said, managers botch career development—and retention—because they mistakenly assume people are satisfied with jobs they excel at. But there are other reasons why career development goes wrong. The first is the way jobs usually get filled, and the second is the fact that career development so often gets handed off to the human resources department.

Most people get moved or promoted in their organizations according to a preset schedule—a new assignment every 18 months, say—or when another position in the company opens up. In either case, managers must scramble. If six employees are all scheduled to get new assignments on August 1, for example, a manager has to play mix and match, and usually does so based on abilities. Who is likely, the manager will ask herself, to do best in which jobs? Similarly, when a position opens up and needs to be filled right away, a manager must ask, "What skills does the job require? Who has them or seems most likely to develop them quickly?"

Sometimes people move up in an organization because they demand it. A talented employee might, for example, inform his manager that he wants to graduate to a new role because he's not growing anymore. The typical manager then considers the employee's skills and tries to find a place in the organization where they can be applied again, this time with a bit of "stretch."

Stretch assignments, however, often do little to address deeply embedded life interests. A research assistant at an investment management firm who performs well can stretch her skills into a credit analyst role, and after continued success there, she can move into the position of fixed-income portfolio manager. But what if her deeper interests are in managing others? Or how about the "spot news" reporter who is "stretched" into management when her real passion (discovered, perhaps, through a few years of misadventure as a manager) lies in investigative reporting?

Skills can be stretched in many directions, but if they are not going in a direction that is congruent with deeply embedded life interests, then employees are at risk of becoming dissatisfied and uncommitted. In such situations, employees usually attribute their unhappiness to their managers or to their organizations. They'll decide their organization has the wrong culture, for example. That kind of thinking often leads to a "migration cure" of leaving one organization for another, only to find similar dissatisfaction because the root of the career malaise has not been identified and addressed. One individual we consulted, a manager in the high-tech industry, went through three companies before realizing it wasn't the company he needed to change but his work. He had never wanted to be a manager but had agreed to a promotion because it offered more money and prestige. All he really wanted to do was design intricate machinery and mechanisms; he wanted to be an engineer again.

That story brings us to the second reason career development is handled poorly. The engineer was originally promoted to manager at the suggestion of the human resources department. Generally speaking, we have found that when career development is handed off to HR, problems arise. Many HR managers try to tackle career development using standardized tests such as the Myers-Briggs Type Indicator. There is nothing wrong with the Myers-Briggs and tests like it. In fact, they are excellent when used to help teams understand their own working dynamics. But personality type should not be the foundation of career development. Some HR managers do use the Strong Interest Inventory to get at life interests, which is better, but it suffers from being too general. The Strong helps people who want to know if they should be a Marine Corps sergeant or a ballet dancer, but it does little for people who say, "I know I want to work in business. Exactly what type of job is best for me?"

The bigger problem with allowing HR to handle career development is that it cuts the manager out of the process. Career development in general, and job sculpting in particular, requires an ongoing dialogue between an employee and his boss; it should not be shunted to another department, however good it may be. HR adds its value in training and supporting managers as career developers.

The Techniques of Job Sculpting

Job sculpting, then, begins when managers identify each employee's deeply embedded life interests. Sometimes an employee's life interest is glaringly obvious—she is excited doing one kind of work and dismal doing another. But much more often, a manager has to probe and observe.

Some managers worry that job sculpting requires them to play psychologist. They shouldn't worry. If they're good managers, they already play the role of psychologist intuitively. Managers *should* have a strong interest in the motivational psychology of their employees. In fact, they should openly express their willingness to help sculpt their employees' careers and to make the extra effort required to hold onto talented people.

Job sculpting, incidentally, can also be marketed externally to attract new hires. We have an unusual vantage point: we've seen close to a thousand new business professionals recruited and hired every year for the last 20 years. Without a doubt, the single most important thing on the minds of new MBAs is—not money!—but whether a position will move their long-term careers in a chosen direction. In fact, during a recent recruiting season, one employer—a Wall Street firm—gained a significant advantage over its competitors by emphasizing its commitment to career development. In both presentations and individual discussions, executives from the firm described its interest in and commitment to helping its professionals think about and manage their careers—a fact that many students cited as key to their choosing that firm.

If managers promise to job sculpt, of course they have to deliver. But how? Each change in assignment provides an opportunity to do some sculpting. For instance, a salesperson with an interest in *quantitative analysis* might be given new duties working with the marketing product manager and market research analysts—while remaining in sales. Or an engineer with an interest in *influence through language and ideas* might be given the task of helping the marketing communications people design sales support materials or user manuals—again, while retaining her primary role as an engineer.

But we have found that such intermittent patching attempts at job sculpting are not nearly as effective as bringing the process directly into the regular performance review. An effective performance review dedicates time to discussing past performance and plans for the future. In making job sculpting part of those conversations, it becomes systematized, and in becoming systematized, the chances of someone's career "falling through the cracks" are minimized.

Do managers need special training to job sculpt? No, but they do need to start listening more carefully when employees describe what they like and dislike about their jobs. Consider the case of a pharmaceutical company executive who managed 30 salespeople. In a performance review, one of her people offhandedly mentioned that her favorite part of the past year had been helping their division find new office space and negotiating for its lease. "That was a blast. I loved it," she told her boss. In the past, the executive would have paid the comment little heed. After all, what did it have to do with the woman's performance in sales? But listening with the ears of a job sculptor, the executive probed further, asking, "What made the search for new office space fun for you?" and "How was that different from what you do day-to-day?" The conversation revealed that the saleswoman was actually very dissatisfied and bored with her current position and was considering leaving. In fact, the saleswoman yearned for work that met her deeply embedded life interests, which had to do with *influence through language and ideas* and *creative production*. Her sales job encompassed the former, but it was only when she had the chance to think about the location, design, and layout of the new office that her creativity could be fully expressed. The manager helped the woman move to a position at company headquarters, where her primary responsibility was to design marketing and advertising materials.

Along with listening carefully and asking probing questions during the performance review, managers can ask employees to play an active role in job sculpting—before the meeting starts. In most corporate settings, the employee's preparation for a performance review includes a written assessment of accomplishments, goals for the upcoming review period, skill areas in need of development, and plans for accomplishing both goals and growth. During the review, this assessment is then compared to the supervisor's assessment.

But imagine what would happen if employees were also expected to write up their personal views of career satisfaction. Imagine if they were to prepare a few paragraphs on what kind of work they love or if they described their favorite activities on the job. Because so many people are unaware of their deeply embedded life interests—not to mention unaccustomed to discussing them with their managers—such exercises might not come easily at first. Yet they would be an excellent starting point for a discussion, ultimately allowing employees to speak more clearly about what they want from work, both in the short and long term. And that information would make even the best job-sculpting managers more effective.

Once managers and employees have discussed deeply embedded life interests, it's time to customize the next work assignment accordingly. In cases where the employee requires only a small change in his activities, that might just mean adding a new responsibility. For example, an engineer who has a deeply embedded life interest in *counseling and mentoring* might be asked to plan and manage the orientation of new hires. Or a logistics planner with a deeply embedded life interest in *influence through language and ideas* could be given the task of working on recruitment at college campuses. The goals here would be to give some immediate gratification through an immediate and real change in the job and to begin the process of moving the individual to a role that more fully satisfies him.

Sometimes, however, job sculpting calls for more substantial changes. Mark, the dissatisfied bank lending officer is one example. Another is Carolyn, who was a star industry analyst at a leading Wall Street firm. Carolyn was so talented at designing and using sophisticated new quantitative approaches to picking stocks that at one point the head of the entire division remarked, "Carolyn has brought our business into the twenty-first century." That same year, she was ranked as the second most valuable person within the entire group—out of almost a hundred very talented finance professionals. For the past several years, senior managers had sought to ensure Carolyn's loyalty to the organization by awarding her generous raises and bonuses, making her one of their highest paid people.

But Carolyn had one foot out the door. When she received a huge raise (even by the standards of this firm and her own compensation history), she was actually angry, commenting to a friend, "That's typical of this company; it thinks that it can solve every problem by throwing money at it." Although she loved analysis and mathematics, she had a strong desire to have a greater impact on the decision making and direction of the research group. She had definite opinions regarding what kind of people they should be hiring, how the group should be organized and the work assigned, and how the group could most effectively work with other departments—in other words, she had deeply embedded life interests in *enterprise control* and *managing people and relationships.*

A performance review gave Carolyn a chance to express her dreams and frustrations to her boss. Together they arrived at a "player-coach" role for Carolyn as coordinator of research. She was still an analyst, but she also had taken on the responsibilities of guiding and directing several teams, making decisions about hiring and promotions, and help ing set strategic direction. A year later, all parties agreed that the research group had never been more productive.

Job sculpting allowed Carolyn's firm to keep some of her extraordinary skills as an analyst while satisfying her desire to manage. But oftentimes job sculpting involves more sacrifice on the part of the organization. Remember that when Mark moved to his new job in business development, the bank lost a talented lending officer. Sometimes job sculpting requires short-term pain for long-term gain, although we would argue that in Mark's case—and in many others like it—they would have lost him soon enough anyway.

And one final caveat emptor. When job sculpting requires taking away parts of a job an employee dislikes, it also means finding someone new to take them on. If staffing levels are sufficient, that won't be a problem— an uninteresting part of one person's job may be perfect for someone else. At other times, however, there won't be a knight in shining armor to take on the "discarded" work. And at still other times, a manager may recognize that there is simply no way to accomplish the job sculpting the employee wants or even needs. (For instance, an engineering firm may not have activities to satisfy a person with a life interest in *influence through language and ideas*.) In such a case, a manager may have to make the hard choice to counsel a talented employee to leave the company.

Even with its challenges, job sculpting is worth the effort. In the knowledge economy, a company's most important asset is the energy and loyalty of its people— the intellectual capital that, unlike machines and factories, can quit and go to work for your competition. And yet, many managers regularly undermine that commitment by allowing talented people to stay in jobs they're doing well at but aren't fundamentally interested in. That just doesn't make sense. To turbo charge retention, you must first know the hearts and minds of your employees and then undertake the tough and rewarding task of sculpting careers that bring joy to both.

The Big Eight

WE HAVE FOUND THAT MOST people in business are motivated by between one and three deeply embedded life interests—long-held, emotionally driven passions for certain kinds of activities. Deeply embedded life interests are not hobbies or enthusiasms; they are innate passions that are intricately entwined with personality. Life interests don't determine what we're good at but what kinds of work we love.

Our conclusions about the number and importance of deeply embedded life interests have grown out of more than a decade of research into the drivers of career satisfaction. In 1986, we began interviewing professionals from a wide range of industries and functions as well as asking them to take a battery of psychological tests in order to assess what factors contributed to work satisfaction. Over the next dozen years, our database had grown to 650 people.

The results of our research were striking: scales on several of the tests we used clearly formed eight separate clusters. In other words, all business work could be broken down into eight types of core activities. By looking more closely at the content of the scales in each cluster and by cross-referencing this information to our interview data and counseling experience, we developed and tested a model of what we call "business core functions." These core functions represent the way deeply embedded life interests find expression in business. The following is a summary of each:

Application of Technology

Whether or not they are actually working as—or were trained to be—engineers, people with the life interest application of technology are intrigued by the inner workings of things. They are curious about finding better ways to use technology to solve business problems. We know a successful money manager who acts as his company's unofficial computer consultant because he loves the challenge of unlocking code. Indeed, he loves it more than his "day job"! People with the application-of-technology life interest often enjoy work that involves planning and analyzing production and operations systems and redesigning business processes.

(continued)

It's often easy to recognize people with a strong application-of-technology life interest. They speak fondly of their college years when they majored in computer science or engineering. They read software magazines and manuals for fun. They comment excitedly when the company installs new hardware.

But sometimes the signs are more subtle. Application-of-technology people often approach business problems with a "let's take this apart and solve it" mind-set. And when introduced to a new process at work, they like to get under the hood and fully understand how it works rather than just turn the key and drive it. In a snapshot, application-of-technology people are the ones who want to know how a clock works because the technology excites them—as does the possibility that it could be tinkered with and perhaps improved.

Quantitative Analysis

Some people aren't just good at running the numbers, they excel at it. They see it as the best, and sometimes the only, way to figure out business solutions. Similarly, they see mathematical work as fun when others consider it drudgery, such as performing a cash-flow analysis, forecasting the future performance of an investment instrument, or figuring out the best debt/equity structure for a business. They might also enjoy building computer models in order to determine optimal production scheduling and to perform accounting procedures.

Not all "quant jocks" are in jobs that reflect this deeply embedded life interest. In fact, many of these individuals find themselves in other kinds of work because they have been told that following their true passion will narrow their career prospects. Yet these people are not difficult to miss, because regardless of their assignment, they gravitate toward numbers. Consider the HR professional who analyzes his organization by looking at compensation levels and benefits and by studying the ratio of managers to employees. Similarly, a marketing manager who loves analyzing customer research data—versus the subjective findings of focus groups—is probably a person with quantitative analysis at her core.

Theory Development and Conceptual Thinking

For some people, nothing brings more enjoyment than thinking and talking about abstract ideas. Think of Mark, the West Coast banker who was frustrated in his position because he did not have the opportunity to ponder big-picture strategy. Like Mark, people with this deeply embedded life interest are drawn to theory—the why of strategy interests them much more than the how. People with this interest can be excited by building business models that explain competition within a given industry or by analyzing the competitive position of a business within a particular market. Our research also shows that people with this deeply embedded interest are often drawn to academic careers. Some end up there; many do not.

How can you identify the people with this interest? For starters, they're not only conversant in the language of theory, but they also genuinely enjoy talking about abstract concepts. Often, these are the people who like thinking about situations from the "30,000 foot" level. Another clue: these individuals often subscribe to periodicals that have an academic bent.

Creative Production

Some people always enjoy the beginning of projects the most, when there are many unknowns and they can make something out of nothing. These individuals are frequently seen as imaginative, out-of-the-box thinkers. They seem most engaged when they are brainstorming or inventing unconventional solutions. Indeed, they seem to thrive on newness. The reason: creative production is one of their dominant deeply embedded life interests—making something original, be it a product or a process.

Our research shows that many entrepreneurs, R&D scientists, and engineers have this life interest. Many of them have an interest in the arts, but just as many don't. An entrepreneur we know has virtually no passion for the arts; his quite successful businesses over the years have included manufacturing decidedly unsexy paper bags and sealing tape.

(continued)

There are, of course, many places in the business world where people with this interest can find satisfying work—new product development, for example, or advertising. Many people with this interest gravitate toward creative industries such as entertainment. Yet others, like one investment analyst we know, repress this life interest because they feel that it is "too soft" for business. Creative production, they believe, is for their off-hours.

Fortunately for managers, most creative-production people are not terribly hard to recognize. They wear their life interest on their sleeves—sometimes literally, by virtue of their choice of unconventional clothing, but almost always by how excited they are when talking about the new elements of a business or product. Oftentimes, they show little interest in things that are already established, no matter how profitable or state-of-the-art.

Counseling and Mentoring

For some people, nothing is more enjoyable than teaching—in business, that usually translates into coaching or mentoring. These individuals are driven by the deeply embedded life interest of counseling and mentoring, allowing them to guide employees, peers, and even clients to better performance. People with a high interest in counseling and mentoring are also often drawn to organizations, such as museums, schools, and hospitals, that provide products or services they perceive to hold a high social value. People like to counsel and mentor for many reasons. Some derive satisfaction when other people succeed; others love the feeling of being needed. Regardless, these people are drawn to work where they can help others grow and improve. We know, for instance, of a brand manager at a consumer goods company who was primarily responsible for designing her product's marketing and distribution plans. Yet she eagerly made time every week to meet one-on-one with several subordinates in order to provide feedback on their performance and answer any questions they had about the company and their careers. When it came time for her performance review, the brand manager's boss didn't bother to evaluate this counseling-and-mentoring work, saying that it wasn't technically part of the brand manager's job. It was, however, her favorite part.

People with a counseling-and-mentoring interest will make themselves known if their jobs include the opportunity to do so. But many people in this category don't get that chance. (New MBAs, in particular, are not asked to coach other employees for several years out.) However, you can sometimes identify counseling-and-mentoring people by their hobbies and volunteer work. Many are drawn to hands-on community service, such as the Big Brother Organization or literacy programs. People with a high interest in counseling and mentoring can be recognized by the fact that when they talk about their previous work they often talk fondly about the people who worked under them and where they are now—like a parent would talk about his or her children.

Managing People and Relationships

Longing to counsel and mentor people is one thing; wanting to manage them is another thing entirely. Individuals with this deeply embedded life interest enjoy dealing with people on a day-to-day basis. They derive a lot of satisfaction from workplace relationships—but they focus much more on outcomes than do people in the counseling-and-mentoring category. In other words, they're less interested in seeing people grow than in working with and through them to accomplish the goals of the business, whether it be building a product or making a sale. That is why people with this life interest often find happiness in line management positions or in sales careers.

Take Tom, a 32-year-old Harvard MBA who joined an Internet start-up in Silicon Valley—mainly because that was what all his classmates were doing. Tom had an undergraduate degree and work experience in engineering, and so his new company put him right to work in its technology division. Tom had no subordinates and no clients and mainly spent his days talking to other engineers and testing prototypes. It was the perfect job for someone with Tom's

(continued)

background, but not for someone with his life interest in managing people and relationships. After six months, he was miserable.

Tom was about to quit when the company announced it needed someone to help set up and run a new manufacturing plant in Texas. Tom pounced on the job—he would ultimately be leading a staff of 300 and negotiating frequently with suppliers. He got the job and still holds it today, five years later. His desire to motivate, organize, and direct people has been happily fulfilled.

Enterprise Control

Sarah, an attorney, is a person who has loved running things ever since she was a child. At age five, she set up her first lemonade stand and refused to let her older brother and sister help pour the juice, set prices, or collect money. (She did, however, let them flag down customers.) As a teenager, Sarah ran a summer camp in her backyard. And in college, she was the president of not one but three major groups, including the student government. People accuse her of being a control freak, and Sarah doesn't argue—she is happiest when she has ultimate decision-making authority. She feels great when she is in charge of making things happen.

Wanting too much control can be unhealthy, both for the people themselves and for their organizations, but some people are driven—in quite healthy ways—by a deeply embedded life interest in enterprise control. Whether or not they like managing people, these people find satisfaction in making the decisions that determine the direction taken by a work team, a business unit, a company division, or an entire organization. Sarah was not particularly happy as a lawyer—a career she pursued at the behest of an influential college instructor, and her mother, a lawyer herself. But she did eventually fulfill her life interest in enterprise control when, after coming back from maternity leave, she asked to run the company's New York office, with 600 attorneys, clerks, and other staff. It was, she says, "a match made in heaven."

Enterprise-control people are easy to spot in organizations. They seem happiest when running projects or teams; they enjoy "owning" a transaction such as a trade or a sale. These individuals also tend to ask for as much responsibility as possible in any work situation. Pure interest in enterprise control can be seen as an interest in deal making or in strategy—a person with this life interest wants to be the CEO, not the COO. Investment bankers, for example, don't run ongoing operations but often demonstrate a very strong interest in enterprise control.

Influence Through Language and Ideas

Some people love ideas for their own sake, but others love expressing them for the sheer enjoyment that comes from storytelling, negotiating, or persuading. Such are people with the deeply embedded life interest of influence through language and ideas. They feel most fulfilled when they are writing or speaking—or both. Just let them communicate.

People in this category sometimes feel drawn to careers in public relations or advertising, but they often find themselves elsewhere, because speaking and writing are largely considered skills, not careers. And yet for some, effective communication is more than just a skill—it's a passion. One way to identify these individuals in your organization is to notice who volunteers for writing assignments. One MBA student we counseled joined a large consulting firm where, for three years, she did the standard analytical work of studying industry dynamics and so forth. When she heard that a partner had to create a report for a new client "that liked to see things in writing," she quickly offered her services. Her report was so persuasive—and she had such a fun experience writing it— that she was soon writing for the company full-time. Had her deeply embedded interest in communication not been met in-house, she surely would have sought it elsewhere.

People with strong interests in influence through language and ideas love persuasion of all sorts, spoken and written, verbal and visual. They enjoy thinking about their audience (whether one person or millions) and the best way to address them. And they enjoy spending time on communications both outside and inside the

(continued)

company. One woman we know who is the head of strategic planning for an entertainment company says, "I spend at least 75% of my time thinking about how to sell our findings to the CEO and other members of the executive team." Clearly, the amount of mental energy this executive devotes to persuasion characterizes her as an influence-through-language-and-ideas person.

As we've noted, it is not uncommon for managers to sense that an employee has more than one deeply embedded life interest. That is possible. The pairs of life interests that are most commonly found together are listed below:

Enterprise Control with Managing People and Relationships. These individuals want to run a business on a day-to-day basis but are also challenged by—and enjoy—managing people.

Managing People and Relationships with Counseling and Mentoring. These are the ultimate people-oriented professionals. They have a strong preference for service-management roles, enjoying the frontline aspects of working in high customer-contact environments. They also tend to enjoy human resources management roles.

Quantitative Analysis with Managing People and Relationships. These individuals like finance and finance-related jobs, yet they also find a lot of pleasure managing people toward goals.

Enterprise Control with Influence Through Language and Ideas. This is the most common profile of people who enjoy sales. (An interest in managing people and relationships is also often high among satisfied salespeople.) This combination is also found extensively among general managers—especially those who are charismatic leaders.

Application of Technology with Managing People and Relationships. This is the engineer, computer scientist, or other technically oriented individual who enjoys leading a team.

Creative Production with Enterprise Control. This is the most common combination among entrepreneurs. These people want to start things and dictate where projects will go. "Give me the ball and I'll score" is their mantra.

TIMOTHY BUTLER and **JAMES WALDROOP** are principals at Peregrine Partners, a consulting firm in Massachusetts.

Originally published in September 1999. Reprint R99502

Let's Hear It for B Players

by Thomas J. DeLong and Vineeta Vijayaraghavan

IN THE MUCH-HERALDED WAR FOR talent, it's hardly surprising that companies have invested a lot of time, money, and energy in hiring and retaining star performers. Most CEOs find that recruiting stars is simply more fun; for one thing, the young A players they interview often remind them of themselves at the same age. For another, their brilliance and drive are infectious; you want to spend time with them. Besides, in these troubled times, when businesses are failing left and right, people who seem to have what it takes to turn a company's performance around are almost irresistible.

But our understandable fascination with star performers can lure us into the dangerous trap of underestimating the vital importance of the supporting actors. A players, it is true, can make enormous contributions to corporate performance. Yet in our collective 20 years of consulting, research, and teaching, we have found that companies' long-term performance—even survival—depends far more on the unsung commitment and contributions of their B players. These capable, steady performers are the best supporting actors of the business world.

Consider Ivan Farmer, a manager who worked on oil rigs for a large conglomerate. (While the stories we discuss here are true, the names are fictitious.) Privately, Ivan was disappointed in his B players for not being "rocket asses," as they are called in the oil business. (Rocket asses shoot up to the top of the corporate hierarchy because they are ready to move anytime, anywhere.) Ivan later openly admitted that he lost respect for his B players because they were less ambitious and, therefore, less like himself and other senior managers. He didn't value their stability; solid B performers stuck with a rig for several years largely because they enjoyed the camaraderie and security of a dependable team.

Unfortunately, many of Ivan's favorite rocket asses flew off to other companies for more money. Many B players also left the company because Ivan so flagrantly disregarded them. The result was that the number of experienced workers on the oil rig fell to dangerously low levels, and the CEO soon began to notice that performance had slipped. In Ivan's struggle to get off the supervisory radar, he realized he had better start valuing and rewarding his solid B engineers.

Companies are routinely blinded to the important role B players serve in saving organizations from themselves. They counterbalance the ambitions of the company's high-performing visionaries whose esteemed strengths, when carried to an extreme, can lead to reckless or volatile behavior. In this sense, B players act as grounders

Idea in Brief

Who's most critical to your company's success, especially during a weak economy? Who supplies the stability, knowledge, and long-term view your firm needs to survive? **B players**—competent, steady performers far from the limelight.

These supporting actors of the corporate world determine your company's future performance far more than A players—volatile stars who may score the biggest revenues or clients, but who're also the most likely to commit missteps. B players, by contrast, prize stability in their work and home lives. They seldom strive for advancement or attention—caring more about their *companies'* well-being. Infrequent job changers, they accumulate deep knowledge about company processes and history. They thus provide ballast during transitions, steadily boosting organizational resilience and performance.

Yet many executives ignore B players, beguiled by stars' brilliance. The danger? If neglected, these dependable contributors may leave, taking the firm's backbone with them. How to keep *your* B players? Recognize their value—and nurture them.

for charismatic A players who might otherwise destabilize the organization. Unfortunately, organizations rarely learn to value their B players in ways that are gratifying for either the company or these employees. As a result, companies see their profits sinking without really understanding why.

This article will help you to rethink the role of your organization's B players—those employees that in a rough ranking are neither the fast-track A players who make up the top 10% nor the struggling C players who make up the bottom 10%. Once you realize your B players' worth, you'll begin to appreciate them more and to

Idea in Practice

The Best B Players

Your most valuable B players are:

- **Former A players.** These highly skilled, focused professionals often jump off the fast track to balance work and family. They continue accomplishing A work—but on their own terms. Seasoned and sharp, they step up during crises.

- **Truth tellers.** Zealously honest in interactions with superiors, they pose challenging questions. Colleagues, recognizing their lack of ambition, highly value their opinions.

- **Go-to managers.** These power brokers compensate for second-rate functional skills with profound understanding of company

processes and norms. They amass such extensive networks that everyone consults them when pushing initiatives through politically challenging terrain.

Corporate Backbone

During turbulent times especially, B players provide stability by:

- **Accumulating organizational memory.** B players remember how their company survived earlier crises—providing indispensable perspective during tough times.

- **Adapting to inevitable change.** Less threatened by restructuring, B performers adapt to change and have the credibility to dispense vital information. They mentor younger

reward them fairly. B performers bring unique strengths to an organization, both every day and in times of crisis, by keeping the company from slipping into entropy. As we'll show, you can mentor and nurture B players to ensure their continued participation in the company. Let's begin by looking at the characteristics of B players your company may be neglecting.

people through the trauma of change, cultivating a reassuring sense of emotional and psychological safety.

- **Staying focused during management shake-ups.** Unlikely to be promoted or fired when a new CEO arrives, B players are usually the most secure people in any company. They ignore political infighting and get back to business, quietly completing projects while A players prepare to jockey for new positions.

Nurturing B Players

To keep your B players motivated:

- **Accept differences.** We're all tougher on people who differ from us. If you're an A player, avoid the temptation to undervalue B performers. Ask what they want from

their careers, then match them with mentors who'll help them get it.

- **Give the gift of time.** Track your communication patterns to ensure you're not ignoring—and thus alienating—solid performers.

- **Hand out the prizes.** Since B players are promoted relatively infrequently, reward them in others ways. Even handwritten notes of appreciation can make them feel valued and motivated.

- **Give choices.** Rather than grooming only stars, allocate scarce resources—compensation, coaching, promotions—to high-potential B players. Promoting sideways can provide appealing career alternatives.

Playing Strong Character Parts

The first truth that companies need to recognize about their B players is that they are not necessarily less intelligent than A players. Achievement is a complicated blend of intelligence, motivation, and personality. As someone once observed of Franklin Roosevelt (a star performer if ever there was one), "He had a second-class mind but a first-class temperament." Research confirms that insight; dozens of psychological studies have demonstrated that A and B players differ at least as much in temperament as intelligence.

So what exactly is the B-player temperament? Perhaps B players' defining characteristic is their aversion to calling attention to themselves—even when they need to. They are like the proverbial wheel that never squeaks—and, consequently, gets no grease. Indeed, we've found that the quickest way of identifying the B players is to list the people who make the fewest demands on the CEO's time. Such reserve is utterly alien to most stars, who make sure that they squeak loudly enough to get the attention they want.

Another pronounced characteristic of B players is that they place a high premium on work-life balance, and they highly value the time they spend with family and friends. Consequently, B players strive for advancement, but not at all costs. Once again, this attitude is anathema to most A players, who relish new opportunities and battles. Indeed, because A players see themselves as stars, they feel less tied to their employers than do B players. At the extreme, they think more about what's good for Brand Me than about what's good for the company.

Like character actors, productive B players tend to assume one of a limited number of distinct organizational types. Perhaps the most productive are *recovered A players* who have rejected the pressures of an A life. For a variety of personal reasons, they have made a conscious decision to drop off the fast track.

Consider Justin Nuckolls. He graduated top of his class at Princeton before winning a Fulbright to study third-world development in Kenya. At 23, Justin was recruited by the American Foreign Service, where he held two major posts by the time he was 30. But Justin soon shifted gears, deciding he didn't want to be a workaholic. He returned to the United States and joined a small publishing firm, where for the last ten years he has been a recovering A player. "I know there are people who look at me today and say that I haven't amounted to much," Justin admits. "What those people don't realize is that there's often as much pleasure in balancing one's whole life as there is in hobnobbing with diplomats and politicians."

Justin Nuckolls isn't alone in wanting something more from his job than glory and a fat paycheck. We've found that individuals who ratchet down their careers because they do not want to be high-powered stars make up about 20% of all B players. Many of these people are tremendously skilled, highly focused professionals in their thirties who have scaled back their ambitions so that they can spend more time with their young families.

Former A players are especially valuable to corporations because they are mobile within the organization. They have "been there" and breathed the rarefied air of A-level performance. They know how A players maneuver and think, and they often continue to accomplish A work—but on their own terms. An A player who values autonomy, for example, will say, "I'm willing to be a B player and do outstanding work for 50 hours a week, but I'm not going to work 80 hours a week no matter how many promotions or how much money you dangle in front of me."

A players who have decided to scale down are a steal for any company, so long as they are correctly managed. Like pinch hitters, they can step up to the plate in times of crisis and bring more to their work when the job requires it. They come equipped with a reservoir of knowledge and wisdom, and the organization is richer because of them.

A second large group of B players consists of *truth tellers*—individuals with an almost religious zeal for honesty and reality in their interactions with superiors. Truth tellers are often functional experts who have carved out a limited but key role for themselves. Typically, they are more interested in their work than in their careers, which means they have the guts to ask in-depth, reflective questions of themselves and others. These B players shatter the myth that all solid players are obedient company types. What's more, because it's widely known that truth tellers aren't ambitious in the usual sense, colleagues don't find them threatening and feel comfortable turning to them for advice.

Take Pete Lassiter, a loner in the trading division of a financial services firm. He is fascinated by his current work at the intersection of technology, trading, and company infrastructure, and he has no desire to be promoted out of his position. Secure in his role, Pete doesn't mince words when he defends the company's values and culture. On one occasion, while traveling to the company's Hong Kong office, he discovered that the office had paid more than the going price for its newly installed computer system. Because the decision to purchase the system had been made by a powerful executive anxious to please a major client, no one had dared to raise any questions. But Pete was in no way cowed by the status of either the client or the executive involved. Pete's courage—which many colleagues described as political naïveté—saved the company millions of dollars.

Another important group of B players consists of managers who may have second-rate functional skills but make up for those deficiencies by developing an extraordinary feel for the organization's processes and norms. We call them the *go-to* people, and their qualities are exemplified by Cindy Friedman, an investment banker who recognized early on that she lacked the analytical skills to shine as a deal maker.

Determined to remain in her high-paying job, Cindy worked hard to become the person others went to when they didn't know whom they should approach or when they had to negotiate difficult political terrain. She managed up with stunning acumen; she developed her networks to such a degree that everyone consulted her when they needed to push something through the organization. As a result, Cindy rose through the ranks, surviving one administration after another and eventually managing bankers far more talented than she was. In a firm where excellence was expected, no one thought Cindy had an A mind—she didn't think so herself. Indeed, she often told her husband that had she been smarter, she never would have become the power broker that she was. Yet the organization undoubtedly got

Why We Work—That Is the Question

WILLIAM BUTLER YEATS once wrote that we all have to choose between perfection of the work and perfection of the life. For Yeats, the idea that there could be a balance between work and life was a fiction. Although Yeats's extreme view does not hold true in Europe, it does in the United States, where a fierce work ethic has imposed a certain rigidity on assumptions about what motivates people on the job. Specifically, the leaders among us often have four misperceptions about employees:

> **Everybody is the same.** Deep down, or so the myth goes, we all have the same goal, to work 24/7 in a way that challenges us uncompromisingly and compels us to continually raise the bar on our performance. Underlying this assumption is the mistaken belief that every employee wants to give his all (or even his best) to the organization, leaving little energy for people and passions outside the workplace.[1]

> **Everybody wants the same thing out of work.** Leaders often assume that all of their followers share their drive for power, status, and money. That's just not so. In fact, the evidence suggests that some people want to influence others in their jobs, others primarily want autonomy, and still others want creative opportunities.

> **Everybody wants to be promoted.** The misconception here is that every employee wants to climb the ladder and rise to corporate prominence. The truth is, many people seek recognition rather than promotion. This difference is critical because our belief that people always want to be promoted is deeply tied to ways that we reward, motivate, hire, and fire them.

> **Everybody wants to be a manager.** Corporate career-planning practices assume that everyone wants to be the boss. Indeed, we typically believe that people will feel rewarded and special if they are given even nominal management responsibilities. For that reason, we often ask people to give up their technical competencies for managerial ones. In the process, unfortunately, we often turn terrific specialists into mediocre managers.

1. For more on this topic, see further work by Lotte Bailyn of MIT's Sloan School of Management.

a lot more done because Cindy was there to make the connections.

We characterize the remaining B players as *middling* because, in general, they are less competent than other B players. Although they are responsible and care deeply about the organization's values, they generally steer clear of risk and aren't entrepreneurial. One classic B player we met during the course of our work managed to stick around in a variety of organizations—and be fairly successful—precisely because she never had an opinion on anything. Nevertheless, middling B players are important. They come closest to being the company's apostles in that they are motivated by the service they can render for the good of the organization. Middling B players feel that they have accomplished something if the company is running like a well-oiled machine. Their own careers take a backseat to the company's well-being.

Oscar-Winning Performances

Like all prize-winning supporting actors, B players bring depth and stability to the companies they work for, slowly but surely improving both corporate performance and organizational resilience. They are always there as quiet yet powerful reminders to high performers obsessed with themselves or as examples to low performers terrified of failure. In that respect, B players counterbalance both ends of the bell curve. They will never garner the most revenue or the biggest clients, but they also will be less likely to embarrass the company or flunk out. They know intuitively how to stay grounded even when their footing may be unsure. And while managers often take this amazing ability for granted, it brings real value to organizations day after day. In times of crisis, B players' stability can be an organization's saving grace.

That stability makes a particularly important contribution to organizational memory. In recent years, a lot has been made of organizational memory, and since B players shift jobs less frequently than A players, chances are they've really seen it all. Because of this long-term perspective, B players can remember when things were as bad before as they are now—and how the company survived. This can prove to be indispensable in tough economic times, when the stage is set for paranoia, blame, and hopelessness.

Take the case of Richard Snow, a truth teller at a New York investment bank. Like all truth tellers, Richard had held a secure, essential position for a long time and posed no threat to higher-ups. During the economic downturn of 2000, therefore, he knew his job was safe. But because he cared deeply about the organization, he reached out to younger colleagues who didn't yet have firsthand experience of how Wall Street firms survived financial crises. Richard's stories brought insight and comfort to the team, reassuring those with shorter organizational memories that things were going to be okay. Like Richard Snow, most B players know through experience that getting back to normal will take time and emotional energy, and in sharing their stories they help move the company toward long-term recovery.

B players not only provide ballast in bad economic times, but they are also less frightened by the possibility of restructuring. They know that change is inevitable; over the years, they've been through a number of major change initiatives, and their historical perspective dampens the volatility that often accompanies these efforts.

When the boss says that things are going to be different around here on Monday morning, B performers are not only able to adapt, but they often also have the credibility with the rest of the organization to share important information and convey a sense of confidence. Even more important, B players have the inner resources to mentor less-experienced people through the transition, stress, and even panic of change—a grossly underestimated talent.

Consider a company that we'll call Scibiolo, a rapidly growing group of biogenetics laboratories that underwent three disruptive change initiatives in five years. After the company's second wave of restructuring, Paul Chung, a promising lab assistant who had just arrived in Los Angeles from Asia, was left without a boss or even a research project. Bruce Jones, a veteran pinch hitter who had once studied in Asia, took Paul under his wing. He put Paul on his team and taught him how the system worked. When a new manager of the lab was eventually put in charge, Paul's potential became clear to everyone. But he always acknowledged that in the midst of chaos and turmoil, Bruce had provided the cultural support that kept the top from spinning off the table.

As a former A player himself, Bruce was well placed to recognize Paul's talent and understand what the young star needed to learn in order to realize his potential. But Bruce's B-player sense of balance kept both of them on the right track. As Bruce put it, "I always knew to pick the foolproof survival strategy: to put our heads down and get to work." Over the years, we have heard the same line from many B players, and we believe that it accounts for the extraordinary sense of emotional and psychological safety we find in many otherwise chaotic organizations.

Beyond the important contribution they make during times of economic turmoil and restructuring, B players have an important balancing role to play in transitions. That's because they are less affected by management shake-ups. By definition, B players are the people passed over for promotions. When a new CEO takes over an organization, A employees prepare to play musical chairs. At the same time, C players burrow deeper into the bowels of the organization to hide their incompetence. But most B players know that they won't likely be promoted—or fired. As the most secure people in the organization, therefore, they are better able to get back to business as usual. Indeed, that's one reason why new CEOs should turn to B players in times of transition. B players know the score but aren't invested in providing a distorted picture of what's been happening.

Clearly, whatever their temperament, B players are strongly influenced by living in the middle of an organization. Left alone, they quietly complete their projects. They put periods at the ends of sentences. They ignore all the political infighting and just get on with their work. And although they may "only" turn out B performances, these players inevitably end up being the backbone of the organization.

Consider a company we'll call Warewick Life Insurance. After the company amassed huge losses, a new CEO assumed leadership. She immediately fired 400 employees and began to rapidly replace people at the top of the company, making an explicit shift in focus away from personal agents to electronic commerce. The organization was in shock—particularly the company's top players who had invested a lot of political capital in the old regime.

During the internal turmoil that ensued, the company's B players brought continuity and calm. While other people wasted hours processing what would happen to them, the job-secure B players raised the strategic question, Would Warewick Life really be able to sell insurance through an impersonal intermediary like a computer? And though most of Warewick's B players still lacked the entrepreneurial skills that had characterized the stars, their years in the middle of the organization had made them organizationally savvy—and independent.

That self-sufficiency paid off. While their new division heads were being appointed, the B players immediately stepped up to the plate and began to manage informally without being asked. Thus, some solid performers automatically took on more responsibility for customer relations, while others took on tasks like teaching computer methods, mentoring, and coaching.

Teaching the Method

Like any employees, no matter how secure and grounded, B players need nurturing and recognition. Without encouragement, they will begin to see themselves as C players. Indeed, organizations often create a vicious cycle in which solid performers are secure enough not to ask for feedback, so leaders focus on high and low performers who need more attention. As a result, B performers stay off the radar and get fewer job opportunities because they're seldom considered in career-planning meetings when possible promotions are discussed.

But without recognition, most B players eventually begin to feel that they're being taken for granted. They disconnect from the soul of the organization and start to look for jobs elsewhere. Losing a solid B performer in this way is a failure for any organization. Yet leaders can do better by their B performers in the following ways:

Accept the Differences

To deal successfully with B players, leaders must first accept that not everyone is like-minded. That's harder than you might think. Psychological studies confirm that we're tougher on people who differ from us than on those we identify with. Since most leaders are themselves highly motivated A players, they tend to undervalue B players who have a different worldview.

Consider what happened to Bob Prince. He led the e-commerce efforts at a large consulting firm during the go-go years of the late 1990s—until the bubble burst. Bob had been handpicked by Ray Cesario, a managing partner of the New York office. Ray wanted Bob to have burn and ambition, but Bob never pushed for more authority, influence, or power. He did his work—and did it well—but he consistently went home at 6 PM.

When Ray began to realize that Bob didn't have the hunger to make it to the top, he dropped him as a protégé. Bob continued to produce very good work, but he suddenly found himself shunned by the rest of the organization. Predictably, Bob received less mentoring and fewer promotions than his more aggressive colleagues. He eventually left the firm, which was forced to spend a lot of money trying to recruit and train a replacement.

That ending was entirely avoidable. For a start, before he hired Bob, Ray should have asked him in detail what he wanted out of his career. This would have helped reveal early on whether there was a fit between Bob, the consulting firm's work culture, and Ray. Once Ray understood Bob's goals, he could have decided to accept Bob on his own grounds, or he could have passed Bob on to a mentor better suited to his career aspirations.

Give the Gift of Time

Even when they think they're being fair, leaders often don't realize how much time they give to their various reports. To be sure that you're not ignoring your solid performers, try tracking your communication patterns. You may be surprised. For instance, Larry Minter, the division head of a leading law firm, learned that certain direct reports were feeling alienated and frustrated because other lawyers were getting more attention than they were. Once Larry was made aware of this, he realized that he didn't even know which lawyers he had been paying more attention to. So Larry began tracking the frequency of his interactions with his direct reports.

A pattern quickly emerged. Certain high-performing partners were always stopping by Larry's office, wanting to express their concerns or just talk. Indeed, several partners who Larry knew were considering leaving the firm began to call on him weekly. Through the course of these meetings, Larry came to understand that these partners just wanted career coaching they could apply elsewhere.

Shockingly, over half of Larry's reports had not initiated any contact with him. They simply went about their work, meeting clients and managing projects and professionals. Larry used the information he received from tracking his interactions to change the way he arranged his schedule. Now Larry makes sure that his day includes regular meetings with *all* his direct reports—including the ones who never ask for special attention.

Hand Out Prizes

Because B performers are promoted less frequently than stars, senior managers should try to reward them in other ways. Indeed, rewarding good performance can be one of the most effective ways to make B players feel more appreciated—and more motivated.

Take the managing editor of a large newspaper. He makes a point of sending handwritten notes to solid performers who have received few accolades. One recipient said that she kept the note she received for more than a year because it made her feel proud of her accomplishments and gave her encouragement.

While gestures such as these are extremely important in the management of B players, that doesn't mean solid B performers need coddling or flattering; they need recognition of their very real contributions. And by the way, leaders needn't worry. The overwhelming majority of B players know that they're not stars. They will be grateful for praise, of course, but most of them won't mistake management attention for elevation to stardom.

Offer Choices

Organizations rarely think about what they can do to retain good performers who don't want to go the usual management route. They typically just ignore the B player until he walks out or gives up and becomes a C player. Sometimes, of course, companies haphazardly fulfill a B player's need for choices. But organizations need to do more than trust their destinies to chance. The challenge is to create a system for allocating scarce resources such as compensation, coaching, and promotions to B performers with the greatest potential.

Consider what we'll call the Princely Hotels, one of India's premier luxury hotel chains. The company's new management created the career development committee, or CDC, in an effort to give opportunities to all managers, not just the stars. Before the CDC was created, high performers were singled out and groomed for advancement. But the chain has more than 60 luxury properties, each needing a general manager that has to be coached. Today the CDC helps B performers get the coaching they need to identify their natural roles and to flourish in them. In particular, the CDC has developed a track for promoting promising employees sideways— thereby offering them genuine career alternatives.

In these and other ways, the CDC ensures that solid
B players do not get lost in the system.

Good movie directors know how important it is to have
consummate actors in supporting roles. Like business's
B players, these actors come in many shapes and sizes.
Some are former A players—think of how many supporting roles have been played by the likes of Alec Guin-
ness and John Gielgud. Others—Kathy Bates, say, or
Frances McDormand—have made particular character
parts their specialty. These players are the truth tellers
of their profession—secure enough to tell the director
what they think but not necessarily interested in secur-
ing the glitziest roles for themselves.

Finally, there are the go-to players of the acting
world, jobbing actors like Kevin Bacon and Ashley Judd
who can play almost any role offered—not brilliantly,
some might say, but not embarrassingly. Such B players
not only make stars like Tom Cruise or Julia Roberts
look better, but they also make the films more than just
vehicles for the star's performance. B players can do the
same for your company, if you have what it takes to foster their particular brand of talent.

THOMAS J. DELONG is a professor of management practice at Harvard Business School.
VINEETA VIJAYARAGHAVAN is a consultant in the New
York office of Katzenbach Partners, an organizational
strategy firm.

Originally published in June 2003. Reprint 4007

Mentoring Millennials

by Jeanne C. Meister and Karie Willyerd

THE MAKEUP OF THE GLOBAL workforce is undergoing a seismic shift: In four years Millennials—the people born between 1977 and 1997—will account for nearly half the employees in the world. In some companies, they already constitute a majority.

That shift may sound daunting to the managers charged with coaching these young workers, who have a reputation for being attention sponges. However, our research into the varying expectations and needs of employees across four generations has given us a more nuanced view of Millennials and uncovered several resource efficient ways to mentor them.

We polled 2,200 professionals across a wide range of industries, asking about their values, their behavior at work, and what they wanted from their employers. The Millennials, we saw, *did* want a constant stream of feedback and *were* in a hurry for success, but their expectations were not as outsized as many assume. That's good news for organizations wondering just who will mentor this rising generation. Baby Boomers are retiring, and Gen X may not be large enough to shoulder the responsibility alone. In the U.S., for instance, the 88 million Millennials vastly outnumber Gen Xers, who are just 50 million strong.

Millennials view work as a key part of life, not a separate activity that needs to be "balanced" by it. For that reason, they place a strong emphasis on finding work that's personally fulfilling. They want work to afford them the opportunity to make new friends, learn new skills, and connect to a larger purpose. That sense of purpose is a key factor in their job satisfaction; according to our research, they're the most socially conscious generation since the 1960s.

"Oh, they want total fulfillment?" managers may be thinking. "Is *that* all?" Yes, Millennials have high expectations of their employers—but they also set high standards for themselves. They've been working on their résumés practically since they were toddlers, because there are so many of them and so few (relatively speaking) spots at top schools and top companies. They're used to overachieving academically and to making strong personal commitments to community service. Keep them engaged, and they will be happy to overachieve for you.

However, they want a road map to success, and they expect their companies to provide it. If you're not careful, grooming them for leadership roles could drain your managers' energy. To help you, we've identified three kinds of mentoring that will prepare Millennials for success without requiring your experienced staffers to spend all their time coaching. While these approaches

Idea in Brief

The makeup of the global workforce is about to undergo a seismic shift. In four years, Millennials—the people born between 1977 and 1997—will account for half the employees in the world. In some companies, they already constitute the majority. That shift may sound daunting to the managers charged with coaching these young workers, who have a reputation for being attention sponges. However, recent research into the varying expectations and needs of employees across four generations, involving 2,200 professionals, offers a more nuanced view of Millennials and reveals several resource-efficient ways to mentor them: reverse mentoring, group mentoring, anonymous feedback, and microfeedback. Using such innovative approaches, companies can give Millennials the guidance that they need—and that they want immediately—without having their experienced managers spend all their time coaching.

will work with employees in other generations, too, they're especially effective with Millennials, because they suit this cohort's mobile, collaborative lifestyle and need for immediacy.

Reverse Mentoring

This approach shifts the responsibility for organizing mentoring to line employees, who learn from senior executives by mentoring *them*. A Millennial is matched to an executive and assigned to teach him or her how to, say, use social media to connect with customers. It's an effective way to give junior employees a window into the higher levels of the organization, so that when the mentees retire, the younger generation has a better understanding of the business.

At Burson-Marsteller, a PR and communications firm with offices in 85 countries, a pilot program of reverse mentoring is bridging experiential divides. The company conducted training for both Millennial mentors and their older mentees, establishing ground rules around confidentiality. "It's difficult not to slip into our traditional roles," says Michele Chase, the managing director of worldwide human resources. "But this arrangement is building relationships. The mentors are getting access to more senior people, and they get to go behind the scenes, so to speak, to see how leaders think and offer insights."

Inevitably, there are times when the older mentees give feedback or advice to their young associates, so in effect, the coaching becomes mutual. The added benefit to the younger workers is a potentially accelerated career track, as the mentoring arrangement raises their profile among senior executives of the firm. And the executive mentees have the opportunity to gain understanding of a segment of their workforce they might not otherwise get to know.

Group Mentoring

Group mentoring is a less-resource-intensive but still effective way of giving Millennials the feedback they crave. It can be led by a more senior manager or can be peer-to-peer, but in both cases, the company sets up a technology platform that allows employees to define mentoring in their own terms.

At AT&T mentoring takes place in self-organizing, topic-based groups, which AT&T calls leadership circles.

The self-organizing approach allows them to reach far more employees than programs run by HR. Using an online platform, one mentor can work with several mentees at a time—sometimes in different locations—on skills like generating sales leads or leading teams. The circles take advantage of platform features such as community forums, document-sharing spaces, group polling, and calendars that announce events and mentor availability. Since the supporting software has some built-in social-networking capability, mentees are able to connect to others with very little hands-on assistance from HR; peer-to-peer mentoring often starts to take place within a circle as it matures. Managers frequently share mentoring responsibilities within a circle—for instance, three executives might work together to advise a group of nine employees. Face-to-face meetings, conference calls, and webcasts supplement the online coaching.

BT, the British telecommunications firm, offers another example of group mentoring: a peer-to-peer learning program it calls Dare2share. "We found 78% of our employees preferred to learn from their peers, but little money or attention was focused on this," explains Peter Butler, the head of learning at BT.

Dare2share is a social collaboration platform that allows employees to pass on their knowledge and insights to their colleagues through short (five- and 10-minute) audio and video podcasts, RSS feeds, and discussion threads, as well as through traditional training documents. BT employees can view content on Dare2share and rate each learning module according to its relevance and quality. If they want to learn more about the topic covered by a module, they can connect with the person who posted it and ask for more information.

Though just out of its four-month proof-of-concept stage, the program is already producing results: New hires now get up to speed more quickly, and training costs have fallen. Among some executives, Dare2share has become the communication tool of choice. For instance, the CEO of one business unit now uses it to report quarterly results via short videos, which give his message broader exposure.

Anonymous Mentoring

This method uses psychological testing and a background review to match mentees with trained mentors outside the organization. Exchanges are conducted entirely online, and both the mentee and the mentor, who is usually a professional coach or seasoned executive, remain anonymous. The engagement, generally paid for by the mentee's company, lasts six to 12 months. In a typical exchange, the mentee might send a message such as this:

> Hey Mentor,
> Tomorrow afternoon I'm presenting our Q4 forecast to the board of directors. I am delivering some bad news and am quite nervous. In fact, I'm VERY nervous! Can you help?

The mentor might respond:

Hey Mentee,

I got your message, and you should know that I have done literally hundreds of presentations—of good news and bad.

When I have bad news, I like to present a benefit/cost analysis of the news. I have found that quantifying it takes away the subjectivity of the message (and the messenger) and allows all parties to focus on what they can do to fix it.

Go there with a mitigation plan, i.e., some potential solutions to your bad news. I have found that boards like to make decisions, so giving them a set of options to choose from is great!

Finally, rehearse your presentation with someone. Let whoever is your audience be very critical of you. That way the real experience will be much easier.

Good luck, and let me know how it went.

One of the mentors we spoke with is Bob Wall, 64, of Connecticut. Having spent 29 years as a consultant and executive coach, he at first couldn't imagine that anonymous mentoring could work. But once he was matched with a mentee, he was amazed at how well they were paired. "I felt like I had a twin out there somewhere," he told us. "It turned out to be a highly intimate relationship while remaining completely anonymous." In fact, "when the six months was up, it was like losing a dear friend."

What Millennials Want

. . . from their boss

Top five characteristics millennials want in a boss:

Will help me navigate my career path

Will give me straight feedback

Will mentor and coach me

Will sponsor me for formal development programs

Is comfortable with flexible schedules

. . . from their company

Top five characteristics millennials want in a company:

Will develop my skills for the future

Has strong values

Offers customizable options in my benefits/reward package

Allows me to blend work with the rest of my life

Offers a clear career path

. . . to learn

Top five things millennials want to learn:

Technical skills in my area of expertise

Self-management and personal productivity

Leadership

Industry or functional knowledge

Creativity and innovation strategies

A Typical Exchange

A TYPICAL EXCHANGE BETWEEN a millennial and his team members using an anonymous online feedback tool

> **Millennial:** "What's one thing I can do to be more successful in my role at the company?"
>
> **Feedback 1:** "Hey, it's Joe, your manager: Ask for more feedback from other members of your team."
>
> **Feedback 2:** "You tend to leave things to the last minute. Plan your time better and start earlier."
>
> **Feedback 3:** "You cut people off when you get excited about your ideas. It comes across as disrespectful whether you mean to be or not."
>
> **Millennial:** "Great suggestions, everyone. Will create a space on our team site where I will post early drafts of my project plan and get your input. I'll demo at our next meeting."

We heard from both mentors and mentees that the anonymity was an unexpected boon. Joanna Sherriff, 33, the vice president of creative services at Decision Toolbox, is just such a mentee. "My original thought was that it would be odd, and it was awkward initially," she says. "In the long run, though, I could see why the anonymity was required. I would never have shared with my mentor some of the things I did if he or she had known my identity or my company."

An additional benefit? Time zones don't matter. Sherriff works from her home in Tauranga, New Zealand, and her mentor was in the United States.

Mentoring with Microfeedback

ONE TOOL THAT CAN SATISFY the thirst for guidance with minimal resources is microfeedback. Think of it as performance assessment for Twitterholics—succinct and nearly real time.

Susan Hutt is now the senior vice president of services and product development at Camilion Solutions, a Toronto-based software company. At her previous job as a senior VP of Workbrain, a San Jose–based software company, she realized she needed to change the way she coached her staff. Millennials made up most of her workforce and, she says, "wanted constant feedback and information on their career progress."

Hutt instituted quarterly reviews and an online, on-demand assessment system that limited feedback to 140 characters. To employees accustomed to instant messaging, texting, and Twitter, the brief advice and suggestions for improvement felt digestible and timely, not curt. The system also allowed them to hear—quickly—from a broad set of people and find out whether they were on the right track. For instance, after an all-hands meeting, an employee could send requests for feedback to five people. "Was it relevant?" they might ask. "Did it cover the content you needed?"

The length limit forces people to think carefully about their responses, and because they must respond so immediately, they're able to provide useful detail. The software involved also collates the responses into a performance dashboard, so employees can track their own private trend lines on skills they are working to improve.

An Edge for the Whole Organization

Improving your company's ability to give employees honest, timely, and useful coaching won't benefit just your 20-something workers. When we asked our survey respondents to rate the importance of eight different managerial skills, respondents in all generations placed a high premium on having a manager who "will give straight feedback." And yet when we asked 300 heads of HR to rate their managers' competence in the same eight skills, giving feedback was ranked dead last. Clearly, that's a critical gap companies need to bridge.

All employees want to feel valued, empowered, and engaged at work. This is a fundamental need, not a generational issue. And, though Gen Xers and Millennials openly discuss and even demand more flexibility in their jobs, Boomers and Traditionalists (also known as the "Silent Generation") want it too, even if they are less vocal about it. You can think of the Millennials as pushing for change that all generations want to see happen.

"Am I continuing to learn and grow?" is a question that resonates with employees of all ages. The way your organization helps them answer that question may be your competitive advantage in attracting, developing, and keeping tomorrow's talent.

JEANNE C. MEISTER and **KARIE WILLYERD** cofounded Future Workplace, a human resources and corporate learning consultancy.

Originally published in May 2010. Reprint R1005D

Off-Ramps and On-Ramps

Keeping Talented Women on
the Road to Success
by Sylvia Ann Hewlett and Carolyn Buck Luce

THROUGHOUT THE PAST YEAR, a noisy debate has erupted in the media over the meaning of what Lisa Belkin of the *New York Times* has called the "opt-out revolution." Recent articles in the *Wall Street Journal,* the *New York Times, Time,* and *Fast Company* all point to a disturbing trend—large numbers of highly qualified women dropping out of mainstream careers. These articles also speculate on what might be behind this new brain drain. Are the complex demands of modern child rearing the nub of the problem? Or should one blame the trend on a failure of female ambition?

The facts and figures in these articles are eye-catching: a survey of the class of 1981 at Stanford University showing that 57% of women graduates leave the work force; a survey of three graduating classes at Harvard Business School demonstrating that only 38% of women graduates end up in full-time careers; and a broader-gauged study of MBAs showing that one in three white women holding an MBA is not working full-time, compared with one in 20 for men with the same degree.

The stories that enliven these articles are also powerful: Brenda Barnes, the former CEO of PepsiCo, who gave up her megawatt career to spend more time with her three children; Karen Hughes, who resigned from her enormously influential job in the Bush White House to go home to Texas to better look after a needy teenage son; and a raft of less prominent women who also said goodbye to their careers. Lisa Beattie Frelinghuysen, for example—featured in a recent *60 Minutes* segment— was building a very successful career as a lawyer. She'd been president of the law review at Stanford and went to work for a prestigious law firm. She quit after she had her first baby three years later.

These stories certainly resonate, but scratch the surface and it quickly becomes clear that there is very little in the way of systematic, rigorous data about the seeming exodus. A sector here, a graduating class there, and a flood of anecdotes: No one seems to know the basic facts. Across professions and across sectors, what is the scope of this opt-out phenomenon? What proportion of professional women take off-ramps rather than continue on their chosen career paths? Are they pushed off or pulled? Which sectors of the economy are most severely affected when women leave the workforce? How many years do women tend to spend out of the workforce? When women decide to reenter, what are they

Idea in Brief

For professional women, it's unusual *not* to step off the career fast track at least once. With children to raise, elderly parents to care for, and other family demands, many women feel they have little choice but to off-ramp.

When women are ready to step back on track, opportunities are limited: Available jobs don't measure up in pay or prestige to previous positions. Result? Women returning to the workforce are demoralized. And companies miss the chance to leverage women's best skills. With talent shortages looming over the next decade, firms must reverse the female brain drain if they hope to beat rivals.

Like it or not, many highly skilled women need to take time off. How to ensure your company's access to their talents over the long term? Help off-ramping women maintain connections that will enable them to reenter the workforce without being marginalized. Reduced-hour jobs, flexible workdays, and removal of off-ramping's stigma are just a few strategies. For example, consulting firm Ernst & Young used such approaches to reverse an expensive downward trend in women's retention and increase its percentage of female partners threefold.

looking for? How easy is it to find on-ramps? What policies and practices help women return to work?

Early in 2004, the Center for Work-Life Policy formed a private sector, multiyear task force entitled "The Hidden Brain Drain: Women and Minorities as Unrealized Assets" to answer these and other questions. In the summer of 2004, three member companies of the task force (Ernst & Young, Goldman Sachs, and Lehman Brothers) sponsored a survey specifically designed to investigate the role of off-ramps and on-ramps in the lives of highly qualified women. The survey, conducted by

Idea in Practice

How to reverse female brain drain in your firm? Consider these strategies.

Create Reduced-Hour Jobs

Offer women ways to keep a hand in their chosen field, short of full-time involvement.

> *Example:* By offering part-time schedules, consumer-products giant Johnson & Johnson boosted employee loyalty and productivity. Female part-time managers maintain they would have quit had part-time jobs not been available. Instead, they push themselves to perform at the same level they achieved before going part-time.

Provide Flexible Workdays

Offer variety in when, where, and how work gets done. A caregiver for an invalid or fragile elderly person may have many hours of potentially productive time in a day, yet not be able to stray far from home.

Provide Flexible Career Arcs

Offer alternative paths that support women during on-ramping and off-ramping phases—so they don't have to quit their career cold turkey.

> *Example:* Management consultancy Booz Allen Hamilton created a pilot "reserve" program for current employees and alumni. It "unbundled" standard management consulting work, identifying bite-sized chunks that could be done via telecommuting or short stints in the office. Then it created a standard employment contract that's activated when chunks of part-time

Harris Interactive, comprised a nationally representative group of highly qualified women, defined as those with a graduate degree, a professional degree, or a high-honors undergraduate degree. The sample size was 2,443 women. The survey focused on two age groups: older women aged 41 to 55 and younger women aged 28 to 40. We also surveyed a smaller group of highly qualified men (653) to allow us to draw comparisons.

work become available. With 150 women employees operating under part-time employment contracts, the company has retained valuable female talent.

Remove the Stigma

Create policies that allow employees to adopt unconventional work arrangements without suffering damage to their careers.

Example: Ernst & Young's chairman made retaining and promoting women a priority. The company equipped all employees for telework and ensured that alternative work schedules didn't affect promotion opportunities. It also created a database of flexible work arrangements. Interested parties learn how arrangements are structured, contact participants with questions, and share lessons learned.

Stop Burning Bridges

Explore off-ramping women's reasons for departing, offering options short of total severance. Clarify that your company's door will remain open to them. And maintain connections with off-ramped employees through formal alumni programs.

Nurture Ambition

Establish "old girls" networks enabling women to build skills, contacts, and confidence, as well as earn recognition. You'll help them sustain their passion for work and their competitive edge.

Using the data from the survey, we've created a more comprehensive and nuanced portrait of women's career paths than has been available to date. Even more important, these data suggest actions that companies can take to ensure that female potential does not go unrealized. Given current demographic and labor market trends, it's imperative that employers learn to reverse this brain drain. Indeed, companies that can develop policies and practices to tap into the female talent pool over the long haul will enjoy a substantial competitive advantage.

Women Do Leave

Many women take an off-ramp at some point on their career highway. Nearly four in ten highly qualified women (37%) report that they have left work voluntarily at some point in their careers. Among women who have children, that statistic rises to 43%.

Factors other than having children that pull women away from their jobs include the demands of caring for elderly parents or other family members (reported by 24%) and personal health issues (9%). Not surprisingly, the pull of elder care responsibilities is particularly strong for women in the 41 to 55 age group—often called the "sandwich" generation, positioned as it is between growing children and aging parents. One in three women in that bracket have left work for some period to spend time caring for family members who are not children. And lurking behind all this is the pervasiveness of a highly traditional division of labor on the home front. In a 2001 survey conducted by the Center for Work-Life Policy, fully 40% of highly qualified women with spouses felt that their husbands create more work around the house than they perform.

Alongside these "pull" factors are a series of "push" factors—that is, features of the job or workplace that make women head for the door. Seventeen percent of women say they took an off-ramp, at least in part, because their jobs were not satisfying or meaningful. Overall, understimulation and lack of opportunity seem to be larger problems than overwork. Only 6% of women stopped working because the work itself was too demanding. In business sectors, the survey results suggest that push factors are particularly powerful—indeed, in these sectors, unlike, say, in medicine or teaching, they outweigh pull factors. Of course, in the hurly-burly world of everyday life, most women are dealing with a combination of push and pull factors—and one often serves to intensify the other. When women feel hemmed in by rigid policies or a glass ceiling, for example, they are much more likely to respond to the pull of family.

It's important to note that, however pulled or pushed, only a relatively privileged group of women have the option of not working. Most women cannot quit their careers unless their spouses earn considerable incomes. Fully 32% of the women surveyed cite the fact that their spouses' income "was sufficient for our family to live on one income" as a reason contributing to their decision to off-ramp.

Contrast this with the experience of highly qualified men, only 24% of whom have taken off-ramps (with no statistical difference between those who are fathers and those who are not). When men leave the workforce, they do it for different reasons. Child-care and elder-care responsibilities are much less important; only 12% of men cite these factors as compared with 44% of women. Instead, on the pull side, they cite switching careers (29%), obtaining additional training (25%), or starting a business (12%) as important reasons for taking time out. For highly qualified men, off-ramping seems to be about strategic repositioning in their careers—a far cry from the dominant concerns of their female peers.

For many women in our study, the decision to off-ramp is a tough one. These women have invested heavily in their education and training. They have spent years accumulating the skills and credentials necessary for successful careers. Most are not eager to toss that painstaking effort aside.

Lost on Reentry

Among women who take off-ramps, the overwhelming majority have every intention of returning to the workforce—and seemingly little idea of just how difficult that will prove. Women, like lawyer Lisa Beattie Frelinghuysen from the *60 Minutes* segment, who happily give up their careers to have children are the exception rather than the rule. In our research, we find that most highly qualified women who are currently off-ramped (93%) want to return to their careers.

Many of these women have financial reasons for wanting to get back to work. Nearly half (46%) cite "having their own independent source of income" as an important propelling factor. Women who participated in focus groups conducted as part of our research talked about their discomfort with "dependence." However good their marriages, many disliked needing to ask for money. Not being able to splurge on some small extravagance or make their own philanthropic choices without clearing it with their husbands did not sit well with them. It's also true that a significant proportion of women currently seeking on-ramps are facing troubling shortfalls in family income: 38% cite "household income no longer sufficient for family needs" and 24% cite "partner's income no longer sufficient for family needs." Given what has happened to the cost of homes (up 38% over the past five years), the cost of college education (up 40% over the past decade), and the cost of health insurance (up 49% since 2000), it's easy to see why many professional families find it hard to manage on one income.

But financial pressure does not tell the whole story. Many of these women find deep pleasure in their chosen careers and want to reconnect with something they love. Forty-three percent cite the "enjoyment and satisfaction" they derive from their careers as an important reason to return—among teachers this figure rises to 54% and among doctors it rises to 70%. A further 16% want to "regain power and status in their profession." In our focus groups, women talked eloquently about how work gives shape and structure to their lives, boosts confidence and self-esteem, and confers status and standing in their communities. For many off-rampers, their professional identities remain their primary identities, despite the fact that they have taken time out.

Perhaps most interesting, 24% of the women currently looking for on-ramps are motivated by "a desire to give something back to society" and are seeking jobs that allow them to contribute to their communities in some way. In our focus groups, off-ramped women

---

How many opt out?

In our survey of highly qualified professionals, we asked the question, "Since you first began working, has there ever been a period where you took a voluntary time out from work?" Nearly four in ten women reported that they had—and that statistic rises to 43% among women who have children. By contrast, only 24% of highly qualified men have taken off-ramps (with no statistical difference between those who are fathers and those who are not).

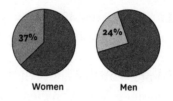

---

talked about how their time at home had changed their aspirations. Whether they had gotten involved in protecting the wetlands, supporting the local library, or rebuilding a playground, they felt newly connected to the importance of what one woman called "the work of care."

Unfortunately, only 74% of off-ramped women who want to rejoin the ranks of the employed manage to do so, according to our survey. And among these, only 40% return to full-time, professional jobs. Many (24%) take part-time jobs, and some (9%) become self-employed. The implication is clear: Off-ramps are around every curve in the road, but once a woman has taken one, on-ramps are few and far between—and extremely costly.

The Penalties of Time Out

Women off-ramp for surprisingly short periods of time— on average, 2.2 years. In business sectors, off-rampers average even shorter periods of time out (1.2 years). However, even these relatively short career interruptions entail heavy financial penalties. Our data show that women lose an average of 18% of their earning power when they take an off-ramp. In business sectors, penalties are particularly draconian: In these fields, women's earning power dips an average of 28% when they take time out. The longer you spend out, the more severe the penalty becomes. Across sectors, women lose a staggering 37% of their earning power when they spend three or more years out of the workforce.

Naomi, 34, is a case in point. In an interview, this part-time working mother was open about her anxieties: "Every day, I think about what I am going to do when I want to return to work full-time. I worry about whether I will be employable—will anyone even look at my résumé?" This is despite an MBA and substantial work experience.

Three years ago, Naomi felt she had no choice but to quit her lucrative position in market research. She had just had a child, and returning to full-time work after the standard maternity leave proved to be well-nigh impossible. Her 55-hour week combined with her husband's 80-hour week didn't leave enough time to raise a healthy child—let alone care for a child who was prone to illness, as theirs was. When her employer denied her request to work reduced hours, Naomi quit.

Why do they leave the fast lane?

Our survey data show that women and men take off-ramps for dramatically different reasons. While men leave the workforce mainly to reposition themselves for a career change, the majority of women off-ramp to attend to responsibilities at home.

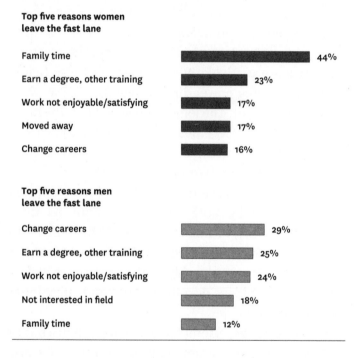

Top five reasons women leave the fast lane

Family time	44%
Earn a degree, other training	23%
Work not enjoyable/satisfying	17%
Moved away	17%
Change careers	16%

Top five reasons men leave the fast lane

Change careers	29%
Earn a degree, other training	25%
Work not enjoyable/satisfying	24%
Not interested in field	18%
Family time	12%

After nine months at home, Naomi did find some flexible work—but it came at a high price. Her new free-lance job as a consultant to an advertising agency barely covered the cost of her son's day care. She now earns a third of what she did three years ago. What plagues Naomi the most about her situation is her anxiety about the future. "Will my skills become obsolete? Will I be able to support myself and my son if something should happen to my husband?"

The scholarly literature shows that Naomi's experience is not unusual. Economist Jane Waldfogel has analyzed the pattern of earnings over the life span. When women enter the workforce in their early and mid twenties they earn nearly as much as men do. For a few years, they almost keep pace. For example, at ages 25 to 29, they earn 87% of the male wage. However, when women start having children, their earnings fall way behind those of men. By the time they reach the 40-to-44 age group, women earn a mere 71% of the male wage. In the words of MIT economist Lester Thurow, "These are the prime years for establishing a successful career. These are the years when hard work has the maximum payoff. They are also the prime years for launching a family. Women who leave the job market during those years may find that they never catch up."

Taking the Scenic Route

A majority (58%) of highly qualified women describe their careers as "nonlinear"—which is to say, they do not follow the conventional trajectory long established by successful men. That ladder of success features a steep gradient in one's 30s and steady progress thereafter. In contrast, these women report that their "career paths have not followed a progression through the hierarchy of an industry."

Some of this nonlinearity is the result of taking off-ramps. But there are many other ways in which women ease out of the professional fast lane. Our survey reveals that 16% of highly qualified women work part-time. Such arrangements are more prevalent in the legal and medical professions, where 23% and 20% of female professionals work less than full-time, than in the business sector, where only 8% of women work part-time. Another common work-life strategy is telecommuting; 8% of highly qualified women work exclusively from home, and another 25% work partly from home.

Looking back over their careers, 36% of highly qualified women say they have worked part-time for some period of time as part of a strategy to balance work and personal life. Twenty-five percent say they have reduced the number of work hours within a full-time job, and 16% say they have declined a promotion. A significant proportion (38%) say they have deliberately chosen a position with fewer responsibilities and lower compensation than they were qualified for, in order to fulfill responsibilities at home.

Downsizing Ambition

Given the tour of women's careers we've just taken, is it any surprise that women find it difficult to claim or sustain ambition? The survey shows that while almost half of the men consider themselves extremely or very ambitious, only about a third of the women do. (The proportion rises among women in business and the professions of law and medicine; there, 43% and 51%, respectively, consider themselves very ambitious.) In a similar vein, only 15% of highly qualified women (and 27% in the business sector) single out "a powerful position" as an important career goal; in fact, this goal ranked lowest in women's priorities in every sector we surveyed.

Far more important to these women are other items on the workplace wish list: the ability to associate with people they respect (82%); the freedom to "be themselves" at work (79%); and the opportunity to be flexible with their schedules (64%). Fully 61% of women consider it extremely or very important to have the opportunity to collaborate with others and work as part of a team. A majority (56%) believe it is very important for them to be able to give back to the community through their work. And 51% find "recognition from my company" either extremely or very important.

These top priorities constitute a departure from the traditional male take on ambition. Moreover, further analysis points to a disturbing age gap. In the business sector, 53% of younger women (ages 28 to 40) own up to being very ambitious, as contrasted with only 37% of older women. This makes sense in light of Anna Fels's groundbreaking work on women and ambition. In a 2004 HBR article, Fels argues convincingly that ambition stands on two legs—mastery and recognition. To hold onto their dreams, not only must women attain the necessary skills and experience, they must also have their achievements appropriately recognized. To the extent the latter is missing in female careers, ambition is undermined. A vicious cycle emerges: As

---

The high cost of time out

Though the average amount of time that women take off from their careers is surprisingly short (less than three years), the salary penalty for doing so is severe. Women who return to the workforce after time out earn significantly less than their peers who remained in their jobs.

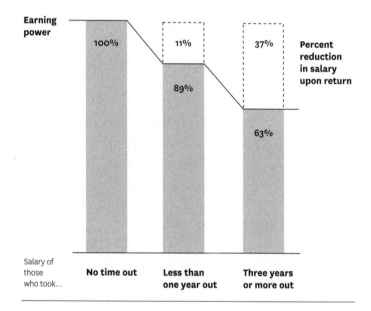

women's ambitions stall, they are perceived as less committed, they no longer get the best assignments, and this lowers their ambitions further.

In our focus groups, we heard the disappointment—and discouragement—of women who had reached senior levels in corporations only to find the glass ceiling still in place, despite years of diversity initiatives. These women feel that they are languishing and have not been given either the opportunities or the recognition that would allow them to realize their full potential. Many feel handicapped in the attainment of their goals. The result is the vicious cycle that Fels describes: a "downsizing" of women's ambition that becomes a self-fulfilling prophecy. And the discrepancy in ambition levels between men and women has an insidious side effect in that it results in insufficient role models for younger women.

Reversing the Brain Drain

These, then, are the hard facts. With them in hand, we move from anecdotes to data—and, more important, to a different, richer analytical understanding of the problem. In the structural issue of off-ramps and on-ramps, we see the mechanism derailing the careers of highly qualified women and also the focal point for making positive change. What are the implications for corporate America? One thing at least seems clear: Employers can no longer pretend that treating women as "men in skirts" will fix their retention problems. Like it or not, large numbers of highly qualified, committed women need to take time out. The trick is to help them maintain connections that will allow them to come back from that time without being marginalized for the rest of their careers.

Create Reduced-Hour Jobs

The most obvious way to stay connected is to offer women with demanding lives a way to keep a hand in their chosen field, short of full-time involvement. Our survey found that, in business sectors, fully 89% of

How Ernst & Young Keeps Women on the Path to Partnership

In the mid-1990s, turnover among female employees at Ernst & Young was much higher than it was among male peers. Company leaders knew something was seriously wrong; for many years, its entering classes of young auditors had been made up of nearly equal numbers of men and women—yet it was still the case that only a tiny percentage of its partnership was female. This was a major problem. Turnover in client-serving roles meant lost continuity on work assignments. And on top of losing talent that the firm had invested in training, E&Y was incurring costs averaging 150% of a departing employee's annual salary just to fill the vacant position.

E&Y set a new course, marked by several important features outlined here. Since E&Y began this work, the percentage of women partners has more than tripled to 12% and the downward trend in retention of women at every level has been reversed. E&Y now has four women on the management board, and many more women are in key operating and client serving roles. Among its women partners, 10% work on a flexible schedule and more than 20 have been promoted to partner while working a reduced schedule. In 2004, 22% of new partners were women.

Focus

Regional pilot projects targeted five areas for improvement: Palo Alto and San Jose focused on life balance, Minneapolis on mentoring, New Jersey on flexible work arrangements, Boston on women networking in the business community, and Washington, DC, on women networking inside E&Y. Successful solutions were rolled out across the firm.

Committed Leadership

Philip Laskawy, E&Y's chairman from 1994 to 2001, made it a priority to retain and promote women. He convened a diversity task force of partners to focus on the problem and created an Office of Retention. Laskawy's successor, Jim Turley, deepened the focus on diversity by rolling out a People First strategy.

Policies

Ernst & Young equipped all its people for telework and made it policy that flexible work schedules would not affect anyone's opportunity for advancement. The new premise was that all jobs could be done flexibly.

New Roles

E&Y's Center for the New Workforce dedicates its staff of seven to developing and advancing women into leadership roles. A strategy team of three professionals addresses the firm's flexibility goals for both men and women. Also, certain partners are designated as "career watchers" and track individual women's progress, in particular, monitoring the caliber of the projects and clients to which they are assigned.

Learning Resources

All employees can use E&Y's Achieving Flexibility Web site to learn about flexible work arrangements. They can track how certain FWAs were negotiated and structured and can use the contact information provided in the database to ask those employees questions about how it is (or isn't) working.

Peer Networking

Professional Women's Networks are active in 41 offices, and they focus on building the skills, confidence, leadership opportunities, and networks necessary for women to be successful. A three-day Women's Leadership Conference is held every 18 months. The most recent was attended by more than 425 women partners, principals, and directors.

Accountability

The annual People Point survey allows employees to rate managers on how well they foster an inclusive, flexible work environment. Managers are also evaluated on metrics like number of women serving key accounts, in key leadership jobs, and in the partner pipeline.

women believe that access to reduced-hour jobs is important. Across all sectors, the figure is 82%.

The Johnson & Johnson family of companies has seen the increased loyalty and productivity that can result from such arrangements. We recently held a focus group with 12 part-time managers at these companies and found a level of commitment that was palpable. The women had logged histories with J&J that ranged from eight to 19 years and spoke of the corporation with great affection. All had a focus on productivity and pushed themselves to deliver at the same level they had achieved before switching to part-time. One woman, a 15-year J&J veteran, was particularly eloquent in her gratitude to the corporation. She had had her first child at age 40 and, like so many new mothers, felt torn apart by the conflicting demands of home and work. In her words, "I thought I only had two choices—work full-time or leave—and I didn't want either. J&J's reduced-hour option has been a savior." All the women in the room were clear on one point: They would have quit had part-time jobs not been available.

At Pfizer, the deal is sweetened further for part-time workers; field sales professionals in the company's Vista Rx division are given access to the same benefits and training as full-time employees but work 60% of the hours (with a corresponding difference in base pay). Many opt for a three-day workweek; others structure their working day around children's school hours. These 230 employees—93% of whom are working mothers—remain eligible for promotion and may return to full-time status at their discretion.

Provide Flexibility in the Day

Some women don't require reduced work hours; they merely need flexibility in when, where, and how they do their work. Even parents who employ nannies or have children in day care, for example, must make time for teacher conferences, medical appointments, volunteering, child-related errands—not to mention the days the nanny calls in sick or the day care center is closed. Someone caring for an invalid or a fragile elderly person may likewise have many hours of potentially productive time in a day yet not be able to stray far from home.

For these and other reasons, almost two-thirds (64%) of the women we surveyed cite flexible work arrangements as being either extremely or very important to them. In fact, by a considerable margin, highly qualified women find flexibility more important than compensation; only 42% say that "earning a lot of money" is an important motivator. In our focus groups, we heard women use terms like "nirvana" and "the golden ring" to describe employment arrangements that allow them to flex their workdays, their workweeks, and their careers. A senior employee who recently joined Lehman Brothers' equity division is an example. She had been working at another financial services company when a Lehman recruiter called. "The person who had been in the job previously was working one day a week from home, so they offered that opportunity to me. Though I was content in my current job," she told us, "that intriguing possibility made me reevaluate. In the end, I took the job at Lehman. Working from home one day a week was a huge lure."

Provide Flexibility in the Arc of a Career

Booz Allen Hamilton, the management and technology consulting firm, recognized that it isn't simply a workday, or a workweek, that needs to be made more flexible. It's the entire arc of a career.

Management consulting as a profession loses twice as many women as men in the middle reaches of career ladders. A big part of the problem is that, perhaps more than in any other business sector, it is driven by an up-or-out ethos; client-serving professionals must progress steadily or fall by the wayside. The strongest contenders make partner through a relentless winnowing process. While many firms take care to make the separations as painless as possible (the chaff, after all, tends to land in organizations that might employ their services), there are clear limits to their patience. Typically, if a valued professional is unable to keep pace with the road warrior lifestyle, the best she can hope for is reassignment to a staff job.

Over the past year, Booz Allen has initiated a "ramp up, ramp down" flexible program to allow professionals to balance work and life and still do the client work they find most interesting. The key to the program is Booz Allen's effort to "unbundle" standard consulting projects and identify chunks that can be done by telecommuting or shorts stints in the office. Participating professionals are either regular employees or alumni that sign standard employment contracts and are activated as needed. For the professional, it's a way to take on a manageable amount of the kind of work they do best. For Booz Allen, it's a way to maintain ties to consultants who have already proved their merit in a challenging profession. Since many of these talented women will eventually return to full-time consulting employment, Booz Allen wants to be their employer of choice—and to keep their skills sharp in the meantime.

When asked how the program is being received, DeAnne Aguirre, a vice president at Booz Allen who was involved in its design (and who is also a member of our task force), had an instant reaction: "I think it's instilled new hope—a lot of young women I work with no longer feel that they will have to sacrifice some precious part of themselves." Aguirre explains that trade-offs are inevitable, but at Booz Allen an off-ramping decision doesn't have to be a devastating one anymore. "Flex careers are bound to be slower than conventional ones, but in ten years' time you probably won't remember the precise year you made partner. The point here is to remain on track and vitally connected."

Remove the Stigma

Making flexible arrangements succeed over the long term is hard work. It means crafting an imaginative set of policies, but even more important, it means eliminating the stigma that is often attached to such nonstandard work arrangements. As many as 35% of the women we surveyed report various aspects of their organizations' cultures that effectively penalize people who take advantage of work-life policies. Telecommuting appears to be most stigmatized, with 39% of women reporting some form of tacit resistance to it, followed by job sharing and part-time work. Of flexible work arrangements in general, 21% report that "there is an unspoken rule at my workplace that people who use these options will not be promoted." Parental leave policies get more respect—though even here, 19% of women report cultural or attitudinal barriers to taking the time off that they are entitled to. In environments where flexible work arrangements are tacitly deemed illegitimate, many women would rather resign than request them.

Interestingly, when it comes to taking advantage of work-life policies, men encounter even more stigma. For example, 48% of the men we surveyed perceived job sharing as illegitimate in their workplace culture—even when it's part of official policy.

Transformation of the corporate culture seems to be a prerequisite for success on the work-life front. Those people at or near the top of an organization need to have that "eureka" moment, when they not only understand the business imperative for imaginative work-life policies but are prepared to embrace them, and in so doing remove the stigma. In the words of Dessa Bokides, treasurer at Pitney Bowes, "Only a leader's devotion to these issues will give others permission to transform conventional career paths."

Stop Burning Bridges
One particularly dramatic finding of our survey deserves special mention: Only 5% of highly qualified women looking for on-ramps are interested in rejoining the companies they left. In business sectors, that percentage is zero. If ever there was a danger signal for corporations, this is it.

The finding implies that the vast majority of off-ramped women, at the moment they left their careers, felt ill-used—or at least underutilized and unappreciated—by their employers. We can only speculate as to why this was. In some cases, perhaps, the situation ended badly; a woman, attempting impossible juggling feats, started dropping balls. Or an employer, embittered by the loss of too many "star" women, lets this one go much too easily.

It's understandable for managers to assume that women leave mainly for "pull" reasons and that there's no point in trying to keep them. Indeed, when family overload and the traditional division of labor place unmanageable demands on a working woman, it does appear that quitting has much more to do with what's going on at home than what's going on at work. However, it is important to realize that even when pull factors seem to be dominant, push factors are also in play. Most off-ramping decisions are conditioned by policies, practices, and attitudes at work. Recognition, flexibility, and the opportunity to telecommute—especially when endorsed by the corporate culture—can make a huge difference.

The point is, managers will not stay in a departing employee's good graces unless they take the time to explore the reasons for off-ramping and are able and willing to offer options short of total severance. If a company wants future access to this talent, it will need to go beyond the perfunctory exit interview and, at the very least, impart the message that the door is open. Better still, it will maintain a connection with off-ramped employees through a formal alumni program.

Provide Outlets for Altruism

Imaginative attachment policies notwithstanding, some women have no interest in returning to their old organizations because their desire to work in their former field has waned. Recall the focus group participants who spoke of a deepened desire to give back to the community after taking a hiatus from work. Remember, too, that women in business sectors are pushed off track more by dissatisfaction with work than pulled by external demands. Our data suggest that fully 52% of women with MBAs in the business sector cite the fact that they do not find their careers "either satisfying or enjoyable" as an important reason for why they left work. Perhaps not surprisingly, then, a majority (54%) of the women looking for on-ramps want to change their profession or field. And in most of those cases, it's a woman who formerly worked in the corporate sphere hoping to move into the not-for-profit sector.

Employers would be well advised to recognize and harness the altruism of these women. Supporting female professionals in their advocacy and public service efforts serves to win their energy and loyalty. Companies may also be able to redirect women's desire to give back to the community by asking them to become involved in mentoring and formal women's networks within the company.

Nurture Ambition

Finally, if women are to sustain their passion for work and their competitive edge—whether or not they take formal time out—they must keep ambition alive. Our findings point to an urgent need to implement mentoring and networking programs that help women expand and sustain their professional aspirations. Companies like American Express, GE, Goldman Sachs, Johnson & Johnson, Lehman Brothers, and Time Warner are developing "old girls networks" that build skills, contacts, and confidence. They link women to inside power brokers and to outside business players and effectively inculcate those precious rainmaking skills.

Networks (with fund-raising and friend-raising functions) can enhance client connections. But they also play another, critical role. They provide the infrastructure within which women can earn recognition, as well as a safe platform from which to blow one's own horn without being perceived as too pushy. In the words of Patricia Fili-Krushel, executive vice president of Time Warner, "Company-sponsored women's networks encourage women to cultivate both sides of the power equation. Women hone their own leadership abilities but also learn to use power on behalf of others. Both skill sets help us increase our pipeline of talented women."

Adopt an On-Ramp

As we write this, market and economic factors, both cyclical and structural, are aligned in ways guaranteed to make talent constraints and skill shortages huge issues again. Unemployment is down and labor markets are beginning to tighten, just as the baby-bust generation is about to hit "prime time" and the number of workers between the ages of 35 to 45 is shrinking. Immigration levels are stable, so there's little chance of relief there. Likewise, productivity improvements are flattening. The phenomenon that bailed us out of our last big labor crunch—the entry for the first time of millions of women into the labor force—is not available to us again. Add it all up, and CEOs are back to wondering how they will find enough high-caliber talent to drive growth.

There is a winning strategy. It revolves around the retention and reattachment of highly qualified women. America these days has a large and impressive pool of female talent. Fifty-eight percent of college graduates are now women, and nearly half of all professional and graduate degrees are earned by women. Even more important, the incremental additions to the talent pool will be disproportionately female, according to figures released by the U.S. Department of Education. The number of women with graduate and professional degrees is projected to grow by 16% over the next decade, while the number of men with these degrees is projected to grow by a mere 1.3%. Companies are beginning to pay attention to these figures. As Melinda Wolfe, head of global leadership and diversity at Goldman Sachs, recently pointed out, "A large part of the potential talent pool consists of females and historically underrepresented groups. With the professional labor market tightening, it is in our direct interest to give serious attention to these matters of retention and reattachment."

In short, the talent is there; the challenge is to create the circumstances that allow businesses to take advantage of it over the long run. To tap this all-important resource, companies must understand the complexities of women's nonlinear careers and be prepared to support rather than punish those who take alternate routes.

Note

The complete statistical findings from this research project, and additional commentary and company examples, are available in an HBR research report entitled "The Hidden Brain Drain: Off-Ramps and On-Ramps in Women's Careers" (see www.womenscareersreport.hbr.org).

SYLVIA ANN HEWLETT is the founder and president of the nonprofit Center for Work-Life Policy in New York. **CAROLYN BUCK LUCE** is the global managing partner for Ernst & Young's health sciences industry practice in New York.

Originally published in March 2005. Reprint R0503B

Making Differences Matter

A New Paradigm for Managing Diversity
by David A. Thomas and Robin J. Ely

WHY SHOULD COMPANIES CONCERN THEMSELVES with diversity? Until recently, many managers answered this question with the assertion that discrimination is wrong, both legally and morally. But today managers are voicing a second notion as well. A more diverse workforce, they say, will increase organizational effectiveness. It will lift morale, bring greater access to new segments of the marketplace, and enhance productivity. In short, they claim, diversity will be good for business.

Yet if this is true—and we believe it is—where are the positive impacts of diversity? Numerous and varied initiatives to increase diversity in corporate America have been under way for more than two decades. Rarely, however, have those efforts spurred leaps in organizational effectiveness. Instead, many attempts to increase diversity in the workplace have backfired, sometimes even heightening tensions among employees and hindering a company's performance.

This article offers an explanation for why diversity efforts are not fulfilling their promise and presents a new paradigm for understanding—and leveraging—diversity. It is our belief that there is a distinct way to unleash the powerful benefits of a diverse workforce. Although these benefits include increased profitability, they go beyond financial measures to encompass learning, creativity, flexibility, organizational and individual growth, and the ability of a company to adjust rapidly and successfully to market changes. The desired transformation, however, requires a fundamental change in the attitudes and behaviors of an organization's leadership. And that will come only when senior managers abandon an underlying and flawed assumption about diversity and replace it with a broader understanding.

Most people assume that workplace diversity is about increasing racial, national, gender, or class representation—in other words, recruiting and retaining more people from traditionally underrepresented "identity groups." Taking this commonly held assumption as a starting point, we set out six years ago to investigate its link to organizational effectiveness. We soon found that thinking of diversity simply in terms of identity-group representation inhibited effectiveness.

Organizations usually take one of two paths in managing diversity. In the name of equality and fairness, they encourage (and expect) women and people of color to blend in. Or they set them apart in jobs that relate specifically to their backgrounds, assigning them, for example, to areas that require them to interface with clients or customers of the same identity group. African

Idea in Brief

You know that workforce diversity is smart business: It opens markets, lifts morale, and enhances productivity. So why do most diversity initiatives backfire—heightening tensions and *hindering* corporate performance?

Many of us simply hire employees with diverse backgrounds—then await the payoff. We don't enable employees' differences to transform *how our organization does work*.

When employees use their differences to shape new goals, processes, leadership approaches, and teams, they bring more of themselves to work. They feel more committed to their jobs—and their companies grow.

How to activate this virtuous cycle? Transcend two existing diversity paradigms: **assimilation** ("we're all the same") or **differentiation** ("we celebrate differences"). Adopt a new paradigm—**integration**—that enables employees' differences to matter.

American M.B.A.'s often find themselves marketing products to inner-city communities; Hispanics frequently market to Hispanics or work for Latin American subsidiaries. In those kinds of cases, companies are operating on the assumption that the main virtue identity groups have to offer is a knowledge of their own people. This assumption is limited—and limiting—and detrimental to diversity efforts.

What we suggest here is that diversity goes beyond increasing the number of different identity-group affiliations on the payroll to recognizing that such an effort is merely the first step in managing a diverse workforce for the organization's utmost benefit. Diversity should be understood as *the varied perspectives and approaches to work* that members of different identity groups bring.

Idea in Practice

	Assimilation Paradigm	Differentiation Paradigm
Premise	"We're all the same."	"We celebrate differences."
Strategy	Hire diverse employees; encourage uniform behavior.	Match diverse employees to niche markets.
Advantage	Promotes fair hiring.	Expands markets.
Disadvantages	Subverting differences to encourage harmony, companies miss out on new ideas. Feeling detached from their work, employees' underperform.	Pigeonholed, staff can't influence mainstream work. Employees feel exploited and excluded from other opportunities.
Example	At a consulting company emphasizing quantitative analysis, minority managers encounter skepticism when they suggest interviewing clients. Labeling the incident as racial discord, the firm doesn't explore the potentially valuable new consulting approach.	To improve oversees operations, a U.S. bank assigns Europeans to its foreign offices. They excel—but the company doesn't know why. Not integrating diversity into its culture and practices, it becomes vulnerable: "If the French team resigns, what will we do?!"

The Integration Paradigm

The **integration paradigm** *transcends* assimilation and differentiation—promoting equal opportunity *and* valuing cultural differences. Result? Employees' diverse perspectives positively impact companies' work.

Example: A public-interest law firm's all-white staff's clients are exclusively white. It hires female attorneys of color, who encourage it to pursue litigation challenging English-only policies. Since such cases didn't fall under traditional affirmative-action work, the firm had ignored them. By taking them, it begins serving more women—immigrants—and enhances the quality of its work. The attorneys of color feel valued, and the firm attracts competent, diverse staff.

Additional suggestions for achieving integration:

1. Encourage open discussion of cultural backgrounds.

   Example: A food company's Chinese chemist draws on her cooking—not her scientific—experience to solve a soup-flavoring problem. But to fit in, she avoids sharing the real source of her inspiration with her colleagues—all white men. Open discussion of cultural differences would engage her more fully in work and workplace relationships.

2. Eliminate all forms of dominance (by hierarchy, function, race, gender, etc.) that inhibit full contribution. When one firm opened its annual strategy conference to people from all hierarchy levels, everyone knew their contributions were valued.

3. Secure organizational trust. In diverse workforces, people share more feelings and ideas. Tensions naturally arise. Demonstrate your commitment to diversity by acknowledging tensions—and resolving them swiftly.

Women, Hispanics, Asian Americans, African Americans, Native Americans—these groups and others outside the mainstream of corporate America don't bring with them just their "insider information." They bring different, important, and competitively relevant knowledge and perspectives about how to actually *do work*—how to design processes, reach goals, frame tasks, create effective teams, communicate ideas, and lead. When allowed to, members of these groups can help companies grow and improve by challenging basic assumptions about an organization's functions, strategies, operations, practices, and procedures. And in doing so, they are able to bring more of their whole selves to the workplace and identify more fully with the work they do, setting in motion a virtuous circle. Certainly, individuals can be expected to contribute to a company their first-hand familiarity with niche markets. But only when companies start thinking about diversity more holistically—as providing fresh and meaningful approaches to work—and stop assuming that diversity relates simply to how a person looks or where he or she comes from, will they be able to reap its full rewards.

Two perspectives have guided most diversity initiatives to date: the *discrimination-and-fairness paradigm* and the *access-and-legitimacy paradigm*. But we have identified a new, emerging approach to this complex management issue. This approach, which we call the *learning-and-effectiveness paradigm,* incorporates aspects of the first two paradigms but goes beyond them by concretely connecting diversity to approaches to work. Our goal is to help business leaders see what their own approach to diversity currently is and how it may already have influenced their companies' diversity efforts. Managers can learn to assess whether they need to change their diversity initiatives and, if so, how to accomplish that change.

The following discussion will also cite several examples of how connecting the new definition of diversity to the actual *doing* of work has led some organizations to markedly better performance. The organizations differ in many ways—none are in the same industry, for instance—but they are united by one similarity: Their leaders realize that increasing demographic variation does not in itself increase organizational effectiveness. They realize that it is *how* a company defines diversity— and *what it does* with the experiences of being a diverse organization—that delivers on the promise.

The Discrimination-and-Fairness Paradigm

Using the discrimination-and-fairness paradigm is perhaps thus far the dominant way of understanding diversity. Leaders who look at diversity through this lens usually focus on equal opportunity, fair treatment, recruitment, and compliance with federal Equal Employment Opportunity requirements. The paradigm's underlying logic can be expressed as follows:

> Prejudice has kept members of certain demographic groups out of organizations such as ours. As a matter of fairness and to comply with federal mandates, we need to work toward restructuring the makeup of our organization to let it more closely reflect that of society. We need managerial processes that ensure that all our employees are treated equally and with respect and that some are not given unfair advantage over others.

Although it resembles the thinking behind traditional affirmative-action efforts, the discrimination-and-fairness paradigm does go beyond a simple concern with numbers. Companies that operate with this philosophical orientation often institute mentoring and career-development programs specifically for the women and people of color in their ranks and train other employees to respect cultural differences. Under this paradigm, nevertheless, progress in diversity is measured by how well the company achieves its recruitment and retention goals rather than by the degree to which conditions in the company allow employees to draw on their personal assets and perspectives to do their work more effectively. The staff, one might say, gets diversified, but the work does not.

What are some of the common characteristics of companies that have used the discrimination-and-fairness paradigm successfully to increase their demographic diversity? Our research indicates that they are usually run by leaders who value due process and equal treatment of all employees and who have the authority to use top-down directives to enforce initiatives based on those attitudes. Such companies are often bureaucratic in structure, with control processes in place for monitoring, measuring, and rewarding individual performance. And finally, they are often organizations with entrenched, easily observable cultures, in which values like fairness are widespread and deeply inculcated and codes of conduct are clear and unambiguous. (Perhaps the most extreme example of an organization in which all these factors are at work is the United States Army.)

Without doubt, there are benefits to this paradigm: it does tend to increase demographic diversity in an organization, and it often succeeds in promoting fair treatment. But it also has significant limitations. The first of these is that its color-blind, gender-blind ideal is to some degree built on the implicit assumption that "we are all the same" or "we aspire to being all the same." Under this paradigm, it is not desirable for diversification of the workforce to influence the organization's work or culture. The company should operate as if every person were of the same race, gender, and nationality. It is unlikely that leaders who manage diversity under this paradigm will explore how people's differences generate a potential diversity of effective ways of working, leading, viewing the market, managing people, and learning.

Not only does the discrimination-and-fairness paradigm insist that everyone is the same, but, with its emphasis on equal treatment, it puts pressure on employees to make sure that important differences among them do not count. Genuine disagreements about work definition, therefore, are sometimes wrongly interpreted through this paradigm's fairness-unfairness lens—especially when honest disagreements are accompanied by tense debate. A female employee who insists, for example, that a company's advertising strategy is not appropriate for all ethnic segments in the marketplace might feel she is violating the code of assimilation upon which the paradigm is built. Moreover, if she were then to defend her opinion by citing, let us say, her personal knowledge of the ethnic group the company wanted to reach, she might risk being perceived as importing inappropriate attitudes into an organization that prides itself on being blind to cultural differences.

Workplace paradigms channel organizational thinking in powerful ways. By limiting the ability of employees to acknowledge openly their work-related but culturally based differences, the paradigm actually undermines the organization's capacity to learn about and improve its own strategies, processes, and practices. And it also keeps people from identifying strongly and personally with their work—a critical source of motivation and self-regulation in any business environment.

As an illustration of the paradigm's weaknesses, consider the case of Iversen Dunham, an international consulting firm that focuses on foreign and domestic economic-development policy. (Like all the examples in this article, the company is real, but its name is disguised.) Not long ago, the firm's managers asked us to help them understand why race relations had become a divisive issue precisely at a time when Iversen was receiving accolades for its diversity efforts. Indeed, other organizations had even begun to use the firm to benchmark their own diversity programs.

Iversen's diversity efforts had begun in the early 1970s, when senior managers decided to pursue greater racial and gender diversity in the firm's higher ranks. (The firm's leaders were strongly committed to the cause of social justice.) Women and people of color were hired and charted on career paths toward becoming project leaders. High performers among those who had left the firm were persuaded to return in senior roles. By 1989, about 50% of Iversen's project leaders and professionals were women, and 30% were people of color. The 13-member management committee, once exclusively white and male, included five women and four people of color. Additionally, Iversen had developed a strong contingent of foreign nationals.

It was at about this time, however, that tensions began to surface. Senior managers found it hard to believe that, after all the effort to create a fair and mutually respectful work community, some staff members could still be claiming that Iversen had racial discrimination problems. The management invited us to study the firm and deliver an outsider's assessment of its problem.

We had been inside the firm for only a short time when it became clear that Iversen's leaders viewed the dynamics of diversity through the lens of the discrimination-and-fairness paradigm. But where they saw racial discord, we discerned clashing approaches to the actual work of consulting. Why? Our research showed that tensions were strongest among midlevel project leaders. Surveys and interviews indicated that white project leaders welcomed demographic diversity as a general sign of progress but that they also thought the new employees were somehow changing the company, pulling it away from its original culture and its mission. Common criticisms were that African American and Hispanic staff made problems too complex by linking issues the organization had traditionally regarded as unrelated and that they brought on projects that seemed to require greater cultural sensitivity. White male project leaders also complained that their peers who were women and people of color were undermining one of Iversen's traditional strengths: its hard-core quantitative orientation. For instance, minority project leaders had suggested that Iversen consultants collect information and seek input from others in the client company besides senior managers—that is, from the rank and file and from middle managers. Some had urged Iversen to expand its consulting approach to include the gathering and analysis of qualitative data through interviewing and observation. Indeed, these project leaders had even challenged one of Iversen's long-standing, core assumptions: that the firm's reports were objective. They urged Iversen Dunham to recognize and address the subjective aspect of its analyses; the firm could, for example, include in its reports to clients dissenting Iversen views, if any existed.

For their part, project leaders who were women and people of color felt that they were not accorded the same level of authority to carry out that work as their white male peers. Moreover, they sensed that those peers were skeptical of their opinions, and they resented that doubts were not voiced openly.

Meanwhile, there also was some concern expressed about tension between white managers and nonwhite subordinates, who claimed they were being treated unfairly. But our analysis suggested that the manager-subordinate conflicts were not numerous enough to warrant the attention they were drawing from top management. We believed it was significant that senior managers found it easier to focus on this second type of conflict than on mid-level conflicts about project choice and project definition. Indeed, Iversen Dunham's focus seemed to be a result of the firm's reliance on its particular diversity paradigm and the emphasis on fairness and equality. It was relatively easy to diagnose problems in light of those concepts and to devise a solution: just get managers to treat their subordinates more fairly.

In contrast, it was difficult to diagnose peer-to-peer tensions in the framework of this model. Such conflicts were about the very nature of Iversen's work, not simply unfair treatment. Yes, they were related to identity-group affiliations, but they were not symptomatic of classic racism. It was Iversen's paradigm that led managers to interpret them as such. Remember, we were asked to assess what was supposed to be a racial discrimination problem. Iversen's discrimination-and-fairness paradigm had created a kind of cognitive blind spot; and, as a result, the company's leadership could not frame the problem accurately or solve it effectively. Instead, the company needed a cultural shift—it needed to grasp what to do with its diversity once it had achieved the numbers. If all Iversen Dunham employees were to contribute to the fullest extent, the company would need a paradigm that would encourage open and explicit discussion of what identity-group differences really mean and how they can be used as sources of individual and organizational effectiveness.

Today, mainly because of senior managers' resistance to such a cultural transformation, Iversen continues to struggle with the tensions arising from the diversity of its workforce.

The Access-and-Legitimacy Paradigm

In the competitive climate of the 1980s and 1990s, a new rhetoric and rationale for managing diversity emerged. If the discrimination-and-fairness paradigm can be said to have idealized assimilation and color- and gender-blind conformism, the access-and-legitimacy paradigm was predicated on the acceptance and celebration of differences. The underlying motivation of the access-and-legitimacy paradigm can be expressed this way:

> We are living in an increasingly multicultural country, and new ethnic groups are quickly gaining consumer power. Our company needs a demographically more diverse workforce to help us gain access to these differentiated segments. We need employees with multilingual skills in order to understand and serve our customers better and to gain legitimacy with them. Diversity isn't just fair; it makes business sense.

Where this paradigm has taken hold, organizations have pushed for access to—and legitimacy with—a more diverse clientele by matching the demographics of the organization to those of critical consumer or constituent groups. In some cases, the effort has led to substantial increases in organizational diversity. In investment banks, for example, municipal finance departments have long led corporate finance departments in pursuing demographic diversity because of the typical makeup of the administration of city halls and county boards. Many consumer-products companies that have used market segmentation based on gender, racial, and other demographic differences have also frequently created dedicated marketing positions for each segment. The paradigm has therefore led to new professional and managerial opportunities for women and people of color.

What are the common characteristics of organizations that have successfully used the access-and-legitimacy paradigm to increase their demographic diversity? There is but one: such companies almost always operate in a business environment in which there is increased diversity among customers, clients, or the labor pool—and therefore a clear opportunity or an imminent threat to the company.

Again, the paradigm has its strengths. Its market-based motivation and the potential for competitive advantage that it suggests are often qualities an entire company can understand and therefore support. But the paradigm is perhaps more notable for its limitations. In their pursuit of niche markets, access-and-legitimacy organizations tend to emphasize the role of cultural differences in a company without really analyzing those differences to see how they actually affect the work that is done. Whereas discrimination-and-fairness leaders are too quick to subvert differences in the interest of preserving harmony, access-and-legitimacy leaders are too quick to push staff with niche capabilities into differentiated pigeonholes without trying to understand what those capabilities really are and how they could be integrated into the company's mainstream work. To illustrate our point, we present the case of Access Capital.

Access Capital International is a U.S. investment bank that in the early 1980s launched an aggressive plan to expand into Europe. Initially, however, Access encountered serious problems opening offices in international markets; the people from the United States who were installed abroad lacked credibility, were ignorant of local cultural norms and market conditions, and simply couldn't seem to connect with native clients. Access responded by hiring Europeans who had attended North American business schools and by assigning them in teams to the foreign offices. This strategy was a marked success. Before long, the leaders of Access could take enormous pride in the fact that their European operations were highly profitable and staffed by a truly international corps of professionals. They took to calling the company "the best investment bank in the world."

Several years passed. Access's foreign offices continued to thrive, but some leaders were beginning to sense that the company was not fully benefiting from its diversity efforts. Indeed, some even suspected that the bank had made itself vulnerable because of how it had chosen to manage diversity. A senior executive from the United States explains:

> If the French team all resigned tomorrow, what would we do? I'm not sure what we *could* do! We've never attempted to learn what these differences and cultural competencies really are, how they change

the process of doing business. What is the German country team actually doing? We don't know. We know they're good, but we don't know the subtleties of how they do what they do. We assumed—and I think correctly—that culture makes a difference, but that's about as far as we went. We hired Europeans with American M.B.A.'s because we didn't know why we couldn't do business in Europe—we just assumed there was something cultural about why we couldn't connect. And ten years later, we still don't know what it is. If we knew, then perhaps we could take it and teach it. Which part of the investment banking process is universal and which part of it draws upon particular cultural competencies? What are the commonalities and differences? I may not be German, but maybe I could do better at understanding what it means to be an American doing business in Germany. Our company's biggest failing is that the department heads in London and the directors of the various country teams have never talked about these cultural identity issues openly. We knew enough to *use* people's cultural strengths, as it were, but we never seemed to learn from them.

Access's story makes an important point about the main limitation of the access-and-legitimacy paradigm: under its influence, the motivation for diversity usually emerges from very immediate and often crisis-oriented needs for access and legitimacy—in this case, the need to broker deals in European markets. However, once the organization appears to be achieving its goal, the leaders seldom go on to identify and analyze the culturally based skills, beliefs, and practices that worked so well. Nor do they consider how the organization can incorporate and learn from those skills, beliefs, or practices in order to capitalize on diversity in the long run.

Under the access-and-legitimacy paradigm, it was as if the bank's country teams had become little spin-off companies in their own right, doing their own exotic, slightly mysterious cultural-diversity thing in a niche market of their own, using competencies that for some reason could not become more fully integrated into the larger organization's understanding of itself. Difference was valued within Access Capital—hence the development of country teams in the first place—but not valued enough that the organization would try to integrate it into the very core of its culture and into its business practices.

Finally, the access-and-legitimacy paradigm can leave some employees feeling exploited. Many organizations using this paradigm have diversified only in those areas in which they interact with particular niche-market segments. In time, many individuals recruited for this function have come to feel devalued and used as they begin to sense that opportunities in other parts of the organization are closed to them. Often the larger organization regards the experience of these employees as more limited or specialized, even though many of them in fact started their careers in the mainstream market before moving to special markets where their cultural backgrounds were a recognized asset. Also, many of these people say that when companies have needed to downsize or narrow their marketing focus, it is the special departments that are often the first to go. That situation creates tenuous and ultimately untenable career paths for employees in the special departments.

The Emerging Paradigm: Connecting Diversity to Work Perspectives

Recently, in the course of our research, we have encountered a small number of organizations that, having relied initially on one of the above paradigms to guide their diversity efforts, have come to believe that they are not making the most of their own pluralism. These organizations, like Access Capital, recognize that employees frequently make decisions and choices at work that draw upon their cultural background—choices made because of their identity-group affiliations. The companies have also developed an outlook on diversity that enables them to *incorporate* employees' perspectives into the main work of the organization and to enhance work by rethinking primary tasks and redefining markets, products, strategies, missions, business practices, and even cultures. Such companies are using the learning-and-effectiveness paradigm for managing diversity and, by doing so, are tapping diversity's true benefits.

A case in point is Dewey & Levin, a small public-interest law firm located in a northeastern U.S. city. Although Dewey & Levin had long been a profitable practice, by the mid-1980s its all-white legal staff had become concerned that the women they represented in employment-related disputes were exclusively white. The firm's attorneys viewed that fact as a deficiency in light of their mandate to advocate on behalf of all women. Using the thinking behind the access-and-legitimacy paradigm, they also saw it as bad for business.

Shortly thereafter, the firm hired a Hispanic female attorney. The partners' hope, simply put, was that she would bring in clients from her own community and also demonstrate the firm's commitment to representing all women. But something even bigger than that happened. The new attorney introduced ideas to Dewey & Levin about what kinds of cases it should take on. Senior managers were open to those ideas and pursued them with great success. More women of color were hired, and they, too, brought fresh perspectives. The firm now pursues cases that its previously all-white legal staff would not have thought relevant or appropriate because the link between the firm's mission and the employment issues involved in the cases would not have been obvious to them. For example, the firm has pursued precedent-setting litigation that challenges English-only policies—an area that it once would have ignored because such policies did not fall under the purview of traditional affirmative-action work. Yet it now sees a link between English-only policies and employment issues for a large group of women—primarily recent immigrants—whom it had previously failed to serve adequately. As one of the white principals explains, the demographic composition of Dewey & Levin "has affected the work in terms of expanding notions of what are [relevant] issues and taking on issues and framing them in creative ways that would have never been done [with an all-white staff]. It's really changed the substance—and in that sense enhanced the quality—of our work."

Dewey & Levin's increased business success has reinforced its commitment to diversity. In addition, people of color at the firm uniformly report feeling respected, not simply "brought along as window dressing." Many of the new attorneys say their perspectives are heard with a kind of openness and interest they have never experienced before in a work setting. Not surprisingly, the firm has had little difficulty attracting and retaining a competent and diverse professional staff.

If the discrimination-and-fairness paradigm is organized around the theme of assimilation—in which the aim is to achieve a demographically representative workforce whose members treat one another exactly the same—then the access-and-legitimacy paradigm can be regarded as coalescing around an almost opposite concept: differentiation, in which the objective is to place different people where their demographic characteristics match those of important constituents and markets.

The emerging paradigm, in contrast to both, organizes itself around the overarching theme of integration. Assimilation goes too far in pursuing sameness. Differentiation, as we have shown, overshoots in the other direction. The new model for managing diversity transcends both. Like the fairness paradigm, it promotes equal opportunity for all individuals. And like the access paradigm, it acknowledges cultural differences among people and recognizes the value in those differences. Yet this new model for managing diversity lets the organization internalize differences among employees so that it learns and grows because of them. Indeed, with the model fully in place, members of the organization can say, We are all on the same team, *with* our differences—not *despite* them.

Eight Preconditions for Making the Paradigm Shift

Dewey & Levin may be atypical in its eagerness to open itself up to change and engage in a long-term transformation process. We remain convinced, however, that unless organizations that are currently in the grip of the other two paradigms can revise their view of diversity so as to avoid cognitive blind spots, opportunities will be missed, tensions will most likely be misdiagnosed, and companies will continue to find the potential benefits of diversity elusive.

Hence the question arises: What is it about the law firm of Dewey & Levin and other emerging third-paradigm companies that enables them to make the most of their diversity? Our research suggests that there are eight preconditions that help to position organizations to use identity-group differences in the service of organizational learning, growth, and renewal.

The Research

THIS ARTICLE IS BASED ON a three-part research effort that began in 1990. Our subject was diversity; but, more specifically, we sought to understand three management challenges under that heading. First, how do organizations successfully achieve and sustain racial and gender diversity in their executive and middle-management ranks? Second, what is the impact of diversity on an organization's practices, processes, and performance? And, finally, how do leaders influence whether diversity becomes an enhancing or detracting element in the organization?

Over the following six years, we worked particularly closely with three organizations that had attained a high degree of demographic diversity: a small urban law firm, a community bank, and a 200-person consulting firm. In addition, we studied nine other companies in varying stages of diversifying their workforces. The group included two financial-services firms, three *Fortune* 500 manufacturing companies, two midsize high-technology companies, a private foundation, and a university medical center. In each case, we based our analysis on interviews, surveys, archival data, and observation. It is from this work that the third paradigm for managing diversity emerged and with it our belief that old and limiting assumptions about the meaning of diversity must be abandoned before its true potential can be realized as a powerful way to increase organizational effectiveness.

1. The leadership must understand that a diverse workforce will embody different perspectives and approaches to work, and must truly value variety of opinion and insight.

We know of a financial services company that once assumed that the only successful sales model was one that utilized aggressive, rapid-fire cold calls. (Indeed, its incentive system rewarded salespeople in large part for the number of calls made.) An internal review of the company's diversity initiatives, however, showed that the company's first-and third-most-profitable employees were women who were most likely to use a sales technique based on the slow but sure building of relationships. The company's top management has now made the link between different identity groups and different approaches to how work gets done and has come to see that there is more than one right way to get positive results.

2. The leadership must recognize both the learning opportunities and the challenges that the expression of different perspectives presents for an organization.
In other words, the second precondition is a leadership that is committed to persevering during the long process of learning and relearning that the new paradigm requires.

3. The organizational culture must create an expectation of high standards of performance from everyone.
Such a culture isn't one that expects less from some employees than from others. Some organizations expect women and people of color to underperform—a negative assumption that too often becomes a self-fulfilling prophecy. To move to the third paradigm, a company must believe that all its members can and should contribute fully.

4. The organizational culture must stimulate personal development.
Such a culture brings out people's full range of useful knowledge and skills—usually through the careful

design of jobs that allow people to grow and develop but also through training and education programs.

5. The organizational culture must encourage openness.
Such a culture instills a high tolerance for debate and supports constructive conflict on work-related matters.

6. The culture must make workers feel valued.
If this precondition is met, workers feel committed to—and empowered within—the organization and therefore feel comfortable taking the initiative to apply their skills and experiences in new ways to enhance their job performance.

7. The organization must have a well-articulated and widely understood mission.
Such a mission enables people to be clear about what the company is trying to accomplish. It grounds and guides discussions about work-related changes that staff members might suggest. Being clear about the company's mission helps keep discussions about work differences from degenerating into debates about the validity of people's perspectives. A clear mission provides a focal point that keeps the discussion centered on accomplishment of goals.

8. The organization must have a relatively egalitarian, nonbureaucratic structure.
It's important to have a structure that promotes the exchange of ideas and welcomes constructive challenges to the usual way of doing things—from any employee

with valuable experience. Forward-thinking leaders in bureaucratic organizations must retain the organization's efficiency-promoting control systems and chains of command while finding ways to reshape the change-resisting mind-set of the classic bureaucratic model. They need to separate the enabling elements of bureaucracy (the ability to get things done) from the disabling elements of bureaucracy (those that create resistance to experimentation).

First Interstate Bank:
A Paradigm Shift in Progress

All eight preconditions do not have to be in place in order to begin a shift from the first or second diversity orientations toward the learning-and-effectiveness paradigm. But most should be. First Interstate Bank, a midsize bank operating in a midwestern city, illustrates this point.

First Interstate, admittedly, is not a typical bank. Its client base is a minority community, and its mission is expressly to serve that base through "the development of a highly talented workforce." The bank is unique in other ways: its leadership welcomes constructive criticism; its structure is relatively egalitarian and nonbureaucratic; and its culture is open-minded. Nevertheless, First Interstate had long enforced a policy that loan officers had to hold college degrees. Those without were hired only for support-staff jobs and were never promoted beyond or outside support functions.

Two years ago, however, the support staff began to challenge the policy. Many of them had been with First

Interstate for many years and, with the company's active support, had improved their skills through training. Others had expanded their skills on the job, again with the bank's encouragement, learning to run credit checks, prepare presentations for clients, and even calculate the algorithms necessary for many loan decisions. As a result, some people on the support staff were doing many of the same tasks as loan officers. Why, then, they wondered, couldn't they receive commensurate rewards in title and compensation?

This questioning led to a series of contentious meetings between the support staff and the bank's senior managers. It soon became clear that the problem called for managing diversity—diversity based not on race or gender but on class. The support personnel were uniformly from lower socioeconomic communities than were the college-educated loan officers. Regardless, the principle was the same as for race-or gender-based diversity problems. The support staff had different ideas about how the work of the bank should be done. They argued that those among them with the requisite skills should be allowed to rise through the ranks to professional positions, and they believed their ideas were not being heard or accepted.

Their beliefs challenged assumptions that the company's leadership had long held about which employees should have the authority to deal with customers and about how much responsibility administrative employees should ultimately receive. In order to take up this challenge, the bank would have to be open to exploring the requirements that a new perspective would impose on it. It would need to consider the possibility of mapping out an educational and career path for people without degrees—a path that could put such workers on the road to becoming loan officers. In other words, the leadership would have to transform itself willingly and embrace fluidity in policies that in times past had been clearly stated and unquestioningly held.

Today the bank's leadership is undergoing just such a transformation. The going, however, is far from easy. The bank's senior managers now must look beyond the tensions and acrimony sparked by the debate over differing work perspectives and consider the bank's new direction an important learning and growth opportunity.

Shift Complete: Third-Paradigm Companies in Action

First Interstate is a shift in progress; but, in addition to Dewey & Levin, there are several organizations we know of for which the shift is complete. In these cases, company leaders have played a critical role as facilitators and tone setters. We have observed in particular that in organizations that have adopted the new perspective, leaders and managers—and, following in their tracks, employees in general—are taking four kinds of action.

They are Making the Mental Connection
First, in organizations that have adopted the new perspective, the leaders are actively seeking opportunities

to explore how identity-group differences affect relationships among workers and affect the way work gets done. They are investing considerable time and energy in understanding how identity-group memberships take on social meanings in the organization and how those meanings manifest themselves in the way work is defined, assigned, and accomplished. When there is no proactive search to understand, then learning from diversity, if it happens at all, can occur only reactively— that is, in response to diversity-related crises.

The situation at Iversen Dunham illustrates the missed opportunities resulting from that scenario. Rather than seeing differences in the way project leaders defined and approached their work as an opportunity to gain new insights and develop new approaches to achieving its mission, the firm remained entrenched in its traditional ways, able to arbitrate such differences only by thinking about what was fair and what was racist. With this quite limited view of the role race can play in an organization, discussions about the topic become fraught with fear and defensiveness, and everyone misses out on insights about how race might influence work in positive ways.

A second case, however, illustrates how some leaders using the new paradigm have been able to envision— and make—the connection between cultural diversity and the company's work. A vice president of Mastiff, a large national insurance company, received a complaint from one of the managers in her unit, an African American man. The manager wanted to demote an African American woman he had hired for a leadership position from another Mastiff division just three months before. He told the vice president he was profoundly disappointed with the performance of his new hire.

"I hired her because I was pretty certain she had tremendous leadership skill," he said. "I knew she had a management style that was very open and empowering. I was also sure she'd have a great impact on the rest of the management team. But she hasn't done any of that."

Surprised, the vice president tried to find out from him what he thought the problem was, but she was not getting any answers that she felt really defined or illuminated the root of the problem. Privately, it puzzled her that someone would decide to demote a 15-year veteran of the company—and a minority woman at that—so soon after bringing her to his unit.

The vice president probed further. In the course of the conversation, the manager happened to mention that he knew the new employee from church and was familiar with the way she handled leadership there and in other community settings. In those less formal situations, he had seen her perform as an extremely effective, sensitive, and influential leader.

That is when the vice president made an interpretive leap. "If that's what you know about her," the vice president said to the manager, "then the question for us is, why can't she bring those skills to work here?" The vice president decided to arrange a meeting with all three present to ask this very question directly. In the meeting, the African American woman explained, "I didn't think I would last long if I acted that way here. My personal style of leadership—that particular style—works well if you have the permission to do it fully; then you can just do it and not have to look over your shoulder."

Pointing to the manager who had planned to fire her, she added, "He's right. The style of leadership I use outside this company can definitely be effective. But I've been at Mastiff for 15 years. I know this organization, and I know if I brought that piece of myself—if I became that authentic—I just wouldn't survive here."

What this example illustrates is that the vice president's learning-and-effectiveness paradigm led her to explore and then make the link between cultural diversity and work style. What was occurring, she realized, was a mismatch between the cultural background of the recently promoted woman and the cultural environment of her work setting. It had little to do with private attitudes or feelings, or gender issues, or some inherent lack of leadership ability. The source of the underperformance was that the newly promoted woman had a certain style and the organization's culture did not support her in expressing it comfortably. The vice president's paradigm led her to ask new questions and to seek out new information, but, more important, it also led her to interpret existing information differently.

The two senior managers began to realize that part of the African American woman's inability to see herself as a leader at work was that she had for so long been undervalued in the organization. And, in a sense, she had become used to splitting herself off from who she was in her own community. In the 15 years she had been at Mastiff, she had done her job well as an individual contributor, but she had never received any signals that her bosses wanted her to draw on her cultural competencies in order to lead effectively.

They are Legitimating Open Discussion

Leaders and managers who have adopted the new paradigm are taking the initiative to "green light" open discussion about how identity-group memberships inform and influence an employee's experience and the organization's behavior. They are encouraging people to make *explicit* use of background cultural experience and the pools of knowledge gained outside the organization to inform and enhance their work. Individuals often do use their cultural competencies at work, but in a closeted, almost embarrassed, way. The unfortunate result is that the opportunity for collective and organizational learning and improvement is lost.

The case of a Chinese woman who worked as a chemist at Torinno Food Company illustrates this point. Linda was part of a product development group at Torinno when a problem arose with the flavoring of a new soup. After the group had made a number of scientific attempts to correct the problem, Linda came up with the solution by "setting aside my chemistry and drawing on my understanding of Chinese cooking." She did not, however, share with her colleagues—all of them white males—the real source of her inspiration for the solution for fear that it would set her apart or that they might consider her unprofessional. Overlaid on the cultural issue, of course, was a gender issue (women cooking) as well as a work-family issue (women doing *home* cooking in a chemistry lab). All of these themes had erected unspoken boundaries that Linda knew could be career-damaging for her to cross. After solving the problem, she simply went back to the so-called scientific way of doing things.

Senior managers at Torinno Foods in fact had made a substantial commitment to diversifying the workforce through a program designed to teach employees to value the contributions of all its members. Yet Linda's perceptions indicate that, in the actual day-to-day context of work, the program had failed—and in precisely one of those areas where it would have been important for it to have worked. It had failed to affirm someone's identity-group experiences as a legitimate source of insight into her work. It is likely that this organization will miss future opportunities to take full advantage of the talent of employees such as Linda. When people believe that they must suggest and apply their ideas covertly, the organization also misses opportunities to discuss, debate, refine, and build on those ideas fully. In addition, because individuals like Linda will continue to think that they must hide parts of themselves in order to fit in, they will find it difficult to engage fully not only in their work but also in their workplace relationships. That kind of situation can breed resentment and misunderstanding, fueling tensions that can further obstruct productive work relationships.

They Actively Work Against Forms of Dominance and Subordination that Inhibit Full Contribution

Companies in which the third paradigm is emerging have leaders and managers who take responsibility for removing the barriers that block employees from using the full range of their competencies, cultural or otherwise. Racism, homophobia, sexism, and sexual harassment are the most obvious forms of dominance that decrease individual and organizational effectiveness—and third-paradigm leaders have zero tolerance for them. In addition, the leaders are aware that organizations can create their own unique patterns of dominance and subordination based on the presumed superiority and entitlement of some groups over others. It is not uncommon, for instance, to find organizations in which one functional area considers itself better than another. Members of the presumed inferior group frequently describe the organization in the very terms used by those who experience identity-group discrimination. Regardless of the source of the oppression, the result is diminished performance and commitment from employees.

What can leaders do to prevent those kinds of behaviors beyond explicitly forbidding any forms of dominance? They can and should test their own assumptions about the competencies of all members of the workforce because negative assumptions are often unconsciously communicated in powerful—albeit nonverbal—ways. For example, senior managers at Delta Manufacturing had for years allowed productivity and quality at their inner-city plants to lag well behind the levels of other plants. When the company's chief executive officer began to question why the problem was never addressed, he came to realize that, in his heart, he had believed that inner-city workers, most of whom were African American or Hispanic, were not capable of doing better than subpar. In the end, the CEO and his senior management team were able to reverse their reasoning and take responsibility for improving the situation. The result was a sharp increase in the performance of the inner-city plants and a message to the entire organization about the capabilities of its entire workforce.

At Mastiff, the insurance company discussed earlier, the vice president and her manager decided to work with the recently promoted African American woman rather than demote her. They realized that their unit was really a pocket inside the larger organization: they did not have to wait for the rest of the organization to make a paradigm shift in order for their particular unit to change. So they met again to think about how to create conditions within their unit that would move the woman toward seeing her leadership position as encompassing all her skills. They assured her that her authentic style of leadership was precisely what they wanted her to bring to the job. They wanted her to be able to use whatever aspects of herself she thought would make her more effective in her work because the whole purpose was to do the job effectively, not to fit some preset traditional formula of how to behave. They let her know that, as a management team, they would try to adjust and change and support her. And they would deal with whatever consequences resulted from her exercising her decision rights in new ways.

Another example of this line of action—working against forms of dominance and subordination to enable full contribution—is the way the CEO of a major chemical company modified the attendance rules for his company's annual strategy conference. In the past, the conference had been attended only by senior executives, a relatively homogeneous group of white men. The company had been working hard on increasing the representation of women and people of color in its ranks, and the CEO could have left it at that. But he reckoned that, unless steps were taken, it would be ten years before the conferences tapped into the insights and perspectives of his newly diverse workforce. So he took the bold step of opening the conference to people from across all levels of the hierarchy, bringing together a diagonal slice of the organization. He also asked the conference organizers to come up with specific interventions, such as small group meetings before the larger session, to ensure that the new attendees would be comfortable enough to enter discussions. The result was that strategy-conference participants heard a much broader, richer, and livelier discussion about future scenarios for the company.

They are Making Sure that Organizational Trust Stays Intact

Few things are faster at killing a shift to a new way of thinking about diversity than feelings of broken trust. Therefore, managers of organizations that are successfully shifting to the learning-and-effectiveness paradigm take one more step: they make sure their organizations remain "safe" places for employees to be themselves. These managers recognize that tensions naturally arise as an organization begins to make room for diversity, starts to experiment with process and product ideas, and learns to reappraise its mission in light of suggestions from newly empowered constituents in the company. But as people put more of themselves out and open up about new feelings and ideas, the dynamics of the learning-and-effectiveness paradigm can produce temporary vulnerabilities. Managers who have helped their organizations make the change successfully have consistently demonstrated their commitment to the process and to all employees by setting a tone of honest discourse, by acknowledging tensions, and by resolving them sensitively and swiftly.

Our research over the past six years indicates that one cardinal limitation is at the root of companies' inability to attain the expected performance benefits of higher levels of diversity: the leadership's vision of the purpose of a diversified workforce. We have described the two most dominant orientations toward diversity and some of their consequences and limitations, together with a new framework for understanding and managing diversity. The learning-and-effectiveness paradigm we have outlined here is, undoubtedly, still in an emergent phase in those few organizations that embody it. We expect that as more organizations take on the challenge of truly engaging their diversity, new and unforeseen dilemmas will arise. Thus, perhaps more than anything else, a shift toward this paradigm requires a high-level commitment to learning more about the environment, structure, and tasks of one's organization, and giving improvement-generating change greater priority than the security of what is familiar. This is not an easy challenge, but we remain convinced that unless organizations take this step, any diversity initiative will fall short of fulfilling its rich promise.

DAVID A. THOMAS is an associate professor at Harvard Business School. **ROBIN J. ELY** is an associate professor at Columbia University's School of International and Public Affairs.

Originally published in September 1996. Reprint 96510

Index

You don't want to miss these...

We've combed through hundreds of *Harvard Business Review* articles on key management topics and selected *the* most important ones to help you maximize your own and your organization's performance.